# Bram Stoker

## Twayne's English Authors Series

Herbert Sussman, Editor

*Northeastern University*

TEAS 343

BRAM STOKER
(1847–1912)

# Bram Stoker

## By Phyllis A. Roth
*Skidmore College*

*Twayne Publishers* • *Boston*

*Bram Stoker*

Phyllis A. Roth

Copyright © 1982 by **G. K.** Hall & Company
Published by Twayne Publishers
A Division of **G. K.** Hall & Company
70 Lincoln Street
Boston, Massachusetts 02111


Book Production by John Amburg
Book Design by Barbara Anderson


Printed on permanent/durable
acid-free paper and bound in
The United States of America.

Library of Congress Cataloging in Publication Data

Roth, Phyllis A.
Bram Stoker.

(Twayne's English authors series; TEAS 343)
Bibliography: p. 157
Includes index.
1. Stoker, Bram, 1847-1912—Criticism and
interpretation. I. Title. II. Series.
PR6037.T617Z83 1982        823'.8        81-13493
ISBN 0-8057-6828-9                          AACR2

For my mother

# Contents

## About the Author

Phyllis A. Roth, associate professor of English at Skidmore College, received her Ph.D. from the University of Connecticut as an N.D.E.A. Title IV Fellow. Author of articles and reviews on the fiction of Vladimir Nabokov, Professor Roth teaches courses in literary theory, Victorian fiction, women's studies, and composition. She has delivered papers at the Modern Language Association Convention on the novels of Charlotte Brontë and Vladimir Nabokov and on Victorian narrative structure, and is a member of the Writing Program at Skidmore, presenting workshops at Networks conferences and serving as a consultant on writing programs for other colleges.

Professor Roth is currently engaged in coediting both a reader of contemporary literary theory and a collection of essays in composition theory and pedagogy, in editing a critical anthology on Vladimir Nabokov, and in a study of narrative symmetry and repetition.

# Preface

Those who know Bram Stoker only as the author of *Dracula* may be startled to learn that he was also the author of a substantial number of short stories, novels and several nonfictional works as well as acting manager for the great English actor, Henry Irving, and one of Irving's first biographers. Indeed, Stoker was extraordinarily dedicated, energetic, and prolific throughout his adult life. Large and striking in appearance, Stoker presided over the productions of the Lyceum Theatre and Henry Irving's American tours alike, serving Irving for some twenty-seven years until the latter's death. It is perhaps all the more surprising, then, to learn that until the age of seven, Stoker was bedridden, unable even to walk. Yet twelve years later, Stoker was University Athlete at Trinity College, Dublin, excelling especially in walking marathons. A few years out of Trinity, Stoker became Irving's assistant in production arrangements, a devotee of the best in British drama, and the author of both a number of potboilers and several more enduring works.

Bram Stoker has nevertheless received little critical attention, except as the author of *Dracula*. In the words of one of his biographers, "Stoker has long remained one of the least known authors of one of the best known books ever written."[1] Two biographies have appeared, both of which suggest some identification between Stoker and Count Dracula. Harry Ludlam's *A Biography of Dracula: The Life Story of Bram Stoker*, published in England in 1962,[2] makes the identification immediately obvious; fortunately, the text is more restrained—indeed, that Ludlam avoids any personal considerations becomes evident once one reads Farson's book. Daniel Farson's *The Man who Wrote Dracula: A biography of Bram Stoker*[3] is more speculative and intimate, adding some privileged family information to which, as Stoker's grandnephew, he

had access, and which he feels may explain Stoker's Count. Together with Stoker's *Personal Reminiscences of Henry Irving*,[4]
these are the major sources of biographical information. Since both
Ludlam and Farson base their material on the *Personal Reminiscences*, the biography of Bram Stoker is to a considerable extent
at the mercy of what Stoker himself chose to record. It may not
be inappropriate, then, though to the countless fans of *Dracula*
it will seem paradoxical, that we know so much of Stoker's work
as Henry Irving's aide and so little of Stoker the author. Stoker
barely mentions his own writing in the *Personal Reminiscences*,
and Ludlam and Farson can only add a few details based mostly
on the chronology of publication. Indeed, Ludlam observes that
*The Times* obituary of Stoker which was only a few column
inches long "was the longest piece ever written about Bram [in
his day], and the last." Its only reference to the fiction was that
" 'Bram Stoker was the master of a particularly lurid and creepy
kind of fiction, represented by *Dracula* and other novels.' " Ludlam indicates further that Stoker is not listed in any encyclopedia
with which he is familiar and that "most of his diaries and personal
papers were lost. He remained in death as he chose to live, sub-
merged in the shadow of Irving."[5]

To this day, little has been written about Stoker, the author.
Moreover, we know only a little of Stoker's writing habits except
that he managed to produce a number of novels and stories while
also fulfilling the awesome responsibilities of acting manager of
the Lyceum Theatre in London. The fiction has stood up surprisingly well in commercial terms for many years; several of the
novels other than *Dracula*, which was in a ninth edition the year
Stoker died, have been reissued a number of times: for example,
*The Jewel of Seven Stars*, *The Lady of the Shroud* (in its twentieth edition by 1934), and *The Lair of the White Worm*.[6] Since
1961, several of the horror tales have been reissued as paperbacks. Additionally, a number of Stoker's short stories have been
anthologized. However, much of Stoker's long fiction and a number of his stories, except for a collection entitled *The Bram Stoker*

*Bedside Companion*,[7] are currently out of print and almost impossible to locate, except in rare book rooms of universities scattered across the country, evidence that to a considerable extent Stoker remains ignored and unknown despite *Dracula*.

More fascinating and complicated than the bibliographical data, though, is the relation between the two sides of Stoker's life—Stoker the prolific if not major author and Stoker the devoted friend and acting manager of Britain's first knighted actor. The following study is the first effort, full-length or otherwise, to analyze the corpus of Stoker's fiction, to suggest relationships between the two major occupations Stoker pursued, and to provide an introduction to the life and work of Bram Stoker. For all texts discussed, I will provide sufficiently detailed story summaries to enable the reader to become familiar with texts which may be difficult to locate. The study will proceed generically rather than strictly chronologically in order to provide an analysis which will best account for the achievement and success of *Dracula*. Moreover, I will trace recurrent themes and preoccupations through the fiction, analyzing narrative strengths and weaknesses and providing the groundwork for a fuller understanding of the facts, fictions, and fantasies of Bram Stoker.

I am indebted to the Rosenbach Museum and Library for permission to quote from the original manuscript in the collection of the Rosenbach Museum and Library, Philadelphia, and to Morton Kaplan, editor of *Literature and Psychology*, for permission to quote from my article, "Suddenly Sexual Women in Bram Stoker's *Dracula*" (1977).

The completion of this book was made possible by the assistance of a number of friends. Grateful acknowledgments go to Professor Herbert Sussman of Northeastern University for many years of support and thoughtfulness; to Eric Weller, Dean of the Faculty, and the members of several Committees on Faculty Research and Grants at Skidmore College whose generous support and encouragement smoothed the rough spots; to Marion Miller whose secretarial and editorial skills are exceeded only by her patience;

to the superb reference librarians at Skidmore College, especially Gloria Moore, Judith Reese, and Patricia Weller; and to Tom.

PHYLLIS A. ROTH

*Skidmore College*

# Chronology

1893   Cruden Bay holiday. Works on *Dracula*.

1895   Henry Irving and W. Thornley Stoker knighted. Extensive tour of U.S. by Lyceum Theatre Company. Meets Theodore Roosevelt.

1896   Continues work on *Dracula* at Cruden Bay. Irving injures his leg.

1897   *Dracula*.

1898   *Miss Betty*. Fire in Lyceum storage buildings.

1899   Irving's health failing.

1900   Irving signs Lyceum over to syndicate.

1901   Death of Charlotte Stoker. Another U.S. tour for Lyceum Company.

1902   Lyceum closes its doors. *The Mystery of the Sea*.

1903   *The Jewel of the Seven Stars*. Ellen Terry leaves the Irving company.

1904   Last U. S. tour.

1905   Death of Henry Irving in Bradford while on provincial tour. Stoker ill. *The Man*.

1906   *Personal Reminiscences of Henry Irving*.

1908   *Lady Athlyne*.

1909   *The Lady of the Shroud*.

1910   *Famous Imposters*. Stoker ill at Cruden Bay but works on *The Lair of the White Worm*.

1911   *The Lair of the White Worm*.

1912   Death of Bram Stoker on 20 April.

## Chapter One
# Bram Stoker: The Life

Born in November of 1847, Bram Stoker was the third of the seven children of Abraham and Charlotte Thornley Stoker. His older brother William called himself W. Thornley Stoker in later years when he was a well-known surgeon, knighted by the queen, and the lover and protector of Florence Dugdale, a woman thirty-five years his junior who was also befriended by the aging Thomas Hardy.[1] The Stokers' second child, Matilda, was a year older than Bram; Tom, Daniel Farson's grandfather, was born two years after Bram and was followed by two more sons, Richard and George, who like the eldest became doctors, and another daughter, Margaret. Information about their childhood is scanty except for two details: Bram's sickliness and his mother's stories. In Stoker's own words, "In my babyhood I used, I understand, to be often at the point of death. Certainly till I was about seven years old, I never knew what it meant to stand upright."[2] One might, then, expect that Bram received the lion's share of attention, and the indications are that he became as devoted to his parents as they seem to have been to him.

Abraham Stoker, twenty years his wife's senior, was a dedicated civil servant who, while he served for more than fifty years as chief secretary at Dublin Castle, received a salary which finally did not suffice to support the family. Described as "a big, fine-looking man,"[3] Abraham passed on his appearance to his namesake.

Bram's mother, Charlotte, was evidently a dynamic personality. Involved in social work before her marriage, she returned to it when her children were grown. Enormously energetic, Charlotte raised her own family and visited, aided, and wrote about the poor, especially about indigent women. Ludlam cites her as writing for the Dublin papers: "The idle and hopeless state of young women in a workhouse renders it the very hotbed of vice, and the experience of years has shown how impossible the task is of providing for them in this country. Avoided and shunned by all classes, we can wonder little when they fall into the lowest depths of vice and wretchedness." Her proposed solution was to "equalize the sexes, both here and in our colonies, by encouraging emigration. In new countries there is a dignity in labor, and a self-supporting woman is alike respected and respectable."[4] Though Charlotte seems not to have specified the means whereby respect was to be achieved in dignified labor, her impulse was, if not feminist, certainly egalitarian. However, this liberality did not extend to her own children. Ludlam reports that "she declared often that she 'did not care tuppence' for her daughters." Undoubtedly, Charlotte transmitted this ambivalence about women to her children.

Possibly as imaginative as her son, Charlotte Stoker recounted Irish tales of superstition, vividly depicting the banshee, whose wail presaged imminent death, as well as the terrors of the cholera epidemic that killed thousands when she was a child in Ireland. Indeed, her description of the latter is virtually a first draft for a story Bram wrote for *Under the Sunset*, a collection of bizarre fairy tales he published years later for his own son, Noel.

Bram's formal childhood education was rounded out by the services of a Dublin tutor, and he had the additional advantage of his father's library, one the modestly paid civil servant kept up despite financial hardship. Moreover, Bram shared with his father a love for theater, discussing with Abraham Stoker the performances of Edmund Kean, who had dominated the Dublin stage thirty years earlier.[5]

In sum, then, Stoker experienced no disadvantage from his childhood invalidism that was evident when he entered Trinity College. In addition to his athletic prowess, he was writing stories and essays by the time he was seventeen, and he became auditor of the Historical Society (equivalent to the presidency of the Union in Oxford or Cambridge) and president of the Philosophical Society where he delivered his first lecture, entitled "Sensationalism in Fiction and Society," an appropriate beginning for him. He graduated Trinity in 1868 with honors in science, later returning for an M.A.

While at Trinity, Stoker enjoyed, as had his father, the special treat of the Theatre Royal in Dublin. The most auspicious theatrical event for Stoker was, of course, the appearance on the Dublin stage of Henry Irving. As Stoker explains at the beginning of his *Personal Reminiscences of Henry Irving*, stock company productions were standard fare. As a result, Henry Irving's performance as Captain Absolute in *The Rivals* was an unusual experience for all theatergoers at the time, Stoker most eloquent and romantic among them: "What I saw, to my amazement and delight, was a patrician figure as real as the person of one's dreams, and endowed with the same poetic grace. A young soldier, handsome, distinguished, self-dependent; compact of grace and slumbrous energy. . . . Such a figure as could only be possible in an age when the answer to insolence was a sword thrust; when only those dare be insolent who could depend to the last on the heart and brain and arm behind the blade" (*PR*, 1:3–4).

Stoker was not to meet Irving for another nine or ten years, though, and, graduating from Trinity, he had to determine on a profession. The only other reported love of his college years was for the poetry of Walt Whitman; however, while Stoker defended *Leaves of Grass* in writing, writing was not something by which he could support himself yet. As a result, he found himself with a clerking job for the civil service obtained for him by his father. After the excitement and success of his college days, Stoker found the clerking tedious in the extreme, finding pleasure and escape only in his essays, writing "several fervid letters to Whitman,"[6] and publicly defending the poet. Years later, while touring the United States with Irving, Stoker met Whitman. Gay Wilson Allen refers to the "semi-love letters to the poet" written by Stoker and reports that after Whitman met both Irving and Stoker, he commented, "best of all was meeting Bram Stoker, the Irish boy who had written so uninhibitedly. . . ."[7]

In 1871 Irving returned to Dublin in *Two Roses*, recreating his London success, and Stoker began slowly albeit unwittingly to shape a career for himself. Discovering that the play, which he had seen three times, received no notice in the Dublin papers, Stoker offered himself to Dr. Henry Maunsell, "Proprietor" of the *Dublin Mail*, as drama critic. While he was encouraged to do the reviews and given "absolutely free hand" (*PR*, 1:13), he was not paid. In addition to his duties at Dublin Castle, therefore, Stoker tutored students in an effort to help his parents pay the debts incurred in educating their sons, but funds were too low for Abraham and Charlotte and the two daughters to be able to remain in Ireland. They determined, therefore, to move to France where they could live at less expense, and Bram moved to lodgings of his own in Kildare Street, Dublin. Chafing further under his dull duties at Dublin Castle, Stoker continued to write without remuneration for the *Mail* and to speak publicly on a variety of topics at Trinity College.[8] Additionally, Stoker took on the editorship of a new newspaper, *The Halfpenny Press*, played in amateur theatricals, and continued his reviews for the *Mail*, successfully influencing Dublin's taste with regard, for example, to the talents of Genevieve Ward, a young woman who had already had one successful career as an opera singer. Around this time also, Stoker published his first horror tale, a serial entitled "The Chain of Destiny," in *The Shamrock* magazine, published in Dublin from 1866 to 1920.

Although making enough to afford a vacation with his family, now living in Zermatt, Stoker felt he had to leave the civil service despite his father's distress at the prospect. Additionally, he mentioned to his father a Miss Henry whom he had met in Paris and for whom he wished to write a play. His father succeeded in talking Bram out of leaving the civil service until he found another means of support. (Miss Henry seems to have been put aside as well.) Bram's compliance with his father's wishes must have been a consolation to him when some months later, Abraham died at Naples at the age of seventy-seven. At this milestone, Charlotte and her daughters elected to remain in Italy for the time; Bram's brothers were all independent; and Bram was just about to realize a dream.

In the fall of 1876, when Bram was twenty-nine, Henry Irving returned to Dublin to present his *Hamlet*, having established his reputation as a leading performer and innovator. Stoker had been writing reviews for five years and on this occasion wrote a glowing tribute to Irving's performance, resulting in Irving's request for an introduction to his admirer. In Stoker's words, "Then began the close friendship between us which only terminated with his life—if indeed friendship, like any other form of love, can ever terminate" (*PR*, 1:25–26). Stoker and Irving took to one another immediately, marking their friendship in a rather extraordinary way. Gathered together after a meal, a small group including Stoker constituted an audience for Irving's recitation of "The Dream of Eugene Aram" by the poet Thomas Hood. Irving's performance was enthralling and devastating, Irving himself "half fainting" and Stoker, "after a few seconds of stony silence following [Irving's] collapse . . . burst[ing] into something like hysterics" (*PR*, 1:31). Irving's gratitude for Stoker's appreciation on this occasion was marked by his presenting his new friend with his photograph, signed: "My dear friend Stoker— God bless you! God bless you!! Henry Irving, Dublin, Dec. 3, 1876." A week later Irving received the combined thanks of Stoker, Trinity College, and the city of Dublin at a university night during which the students, who had taken over the theater for the evening's performance, presented a speech of gratitude written by Stoker.

Not surprisingly, when Irving left Dublin after this tour, Stoker was even unhappier with his situation in Dublin Castle. However, he was at this time promoted to a position as an inspector of Petty Sessions which varied the routine by requiring his presence in the courts. Evidently, too, the new work was sufficiently engaging so that he resigned his post as drama critic and began work on a very different writing task, a rule book—described by Stoker himself as "dry-as-dust" (*PR*, 1:32)—for the clerks of the Petty Sessions: "a complete guide to a clerk's daily duties, from how

best to tot up accounts to how to collect fines, deal with dangerous idiots, debts, deserters, trespassing cattle and discovery of
arms."[9] When completed in September 1879, the book was called
*The Duties of the Clerks of Petty Sessions in Ireland.*

In June of 1877 Irving returned to Dublin for a reading,
bringing with him his new stage manager, Harry J. Loveday,
whom he introduced to Stoker. Several weeks later Bram joined
the two in London for a brief vacation. Three months later, Irving was back in Dublin with plans for his own theater in London,
plans which would call for an acting manager. During the time
required for these plans to come to fruition, Stoker was again in
London—in June of 1878—this time helping Irving rework the
script of a version of *The Flying Dutchman.* Irving returned to
Dublin both in August (for a benefit reading for a Belfast hospital) and September of 1878. These were clearly delightful
times for both men and their friends. In Stoker's words, "we
drove almost every day and dined and supped at the house of my
brother [W. Thornley Stoker] and sister-in-law, with whom he
was great friends; at my own lodgings or his hotel; at restaurants
or in the house of other friends. . . . We had now been close
friends for over two years. We understood each other's nature,
needs and ambitions, and had a mutual confidence . . . rare amongst
men" (*PR*, 1:60).

In November Irving was able to get the lease of the Lyceum
Theatre and form his own company. When he did, he immediately telegraphed Stoker to join him in Glasgow where Irving
offered him the position as acting manager that Stoker was to fill
so ably for the next twenty-seven years. Farson comments, "If
Stoker was to attach himself to the promise of another, he chose
the best in Irving: an autocrat, a complex character, and in many
ways a selfish man, but infinitely rewarding through his work."[10]

Stoker's life was settled in another way as well by the time
he arrived at the Lyceum in December 1878; he had been married
for five days. About a year earlier the family of Lieutenant-Colonel
James Balcombe had moved into a house next door to Stoker's
on Harcourt Street, and Bram attached himself to the third of

the five daughters, nineteen-year-old Florence, whom Ludlam portrays as awed by Stoker's theatrical connections and delighted by his anecdotes.[11] The marriage took place in Dublin on 4 December and Florence journeyed to London with Bram. Ludlam mentions Florence only in passing in the rest of his biography, the effect of which is most decidedly to keep her in an extremely subordinate position to Irving. Some conflict exists in these accounts of Florence, and it is not entirely clear how long Stoker had known Florence when he married her. According to Farson, Florence was an extraordinarily beautiful woman who had known Stoker for a number of years before they married. Stoker himself makes it evident that he and Florence were already engaged when Irving called for him; they simply married earlier than planned (*PR*, 1:61).

Farson also reports that he received from Noel Stoker, the only child of Florence and Bram, a "sack of letters" including letters to Florence from Oscar Wilde who was evidently enamored of her and angered by her marriage to Stoker. Nevertheless, Wilde remained a visitor of both Stokers when they moved into 27 Cheyne Walk, a fashionable private house where they held "at homes" on Sundays attended by many famous people Stoker met through Irving. "It was not just the quantity but the variety of 'names' that made [their] world so interesting: heads of state; . . . the young Ethel Barrymore asking for an audition; Barrie, Pinero; Arthur Conon Doyle"; the explorer H. M. Stanley; Sir Richard and Lady Burton, all frequented the Lyceum. The Stokers also entertained Mark Twain, G. S. Gilbert, Lord and Lady Tennyson. Farson claims, in fact, that with Stoker Florence was able to realize the aspirations of a "vaulting social ambition,"[12] an ambition he says that made her an indifferent mother.

When Stoker arrived to assume his duties on 15 December, the state of affairs at the Lyceum was intimidating. The theater was being completely redecorated both inside and out, all new properties and sets had been ordered for the production of *Hamlet* scheduled to open just two weeks later on the thirtieth, and Irving had effected a £12,000 overdraft, most of which monies had

already been disbursed. Nevertheless, Stoker took hold and organized his staff and responsibilities, the first season totaling receipts
of £36,000 by the end of Stoker's first seven months.

Stoker's first full year with Irving was notable for many reasons.
Not only was he instrumental in the brilliant opening of Henry
Irving's Lyceum Theatre, appearing on opening night as the
"red-haired giant" in dress suit (as he was often called) presid-
ing over the house, the performance, and the celebrations—as
was the tradition—but he was responsible for another dramatic
success during the summer months. Irving had leased the theater
to the actress Genevieve Ward whom Stoker had admired years
before. Her choice of Zillah to open with was disastrous, and
Stoker was responsible for selecting for her as its replacement a
play called Forget-Me-Not by Herman Merivale and F. C. Grove.
The play apparently made Miss Ward's career and she performed
in it over 2,000 times in ten years with great financial success.

During Miss Ward's lease of the Lyceum, Stoker restored a set
of rooms at the back of the theater to their original function as a
dining and entertaining suite. Almost a century earlier, these rooms
had been "the meeting place of the Sublime Society of Beefsteaks,
whose membership had included Sheridan, Lord Erskine, and
the Duke of Norfolk."[13] And, thanks to Stoker, the aftertheater
dinners in the Beefsteak Room became an exciting and esteemed
part of theater life in London. Stoker's accomplishments of the
year were capped by the birth of his son, Noel, on 29 December.

The degree of activity in which Stoker was engaged in 1879
was consistent with earlier years and formed a model for the
rest of his years with Irving. As Farson describes it, "Bram's
capacity for work was abnormal: throughout his life he ran two
careers simultaneously, wrote scores of letters in his own hand,
at one time several hundred a week [Irving's correspondence],
and enjoyed that Victorian ability to maintain friendship which
we seem to have lost. And even then, as if he had a surplus of
energy, he set out on marathon walking tours."[14]

The energy devoted to Irving's service was extended to all
the players of the company as well, particularly to Irving's lead-

ing lady, Ellen Terry. Ludlam indicates that Stoker's devotion to her dated from their first meeting. She was an extraordinarily charismatic woman and actress. According to Farson, "she was devoid of envy . . . a generous artist [who] did not share the high opinion in which she was held by everyone else." She depended upon Stoker, calling him "Ma" and "Mama," relying on him equally for advice on stocks, small loans, tickets for friends, and proper material for costumes. Married three times—each marriage as unusual as the others—Ellen Terry was Irving's theater partner for twenty years, through twenty-seven productions. It is conjectured that Terry and Irving may have been lovers, but their behavior was so discreet that they excited little gossip. Indeed, Ellen Terry and her third husband were received most graciously by Queen Victoria, and in 1925, at the end of her life, Ellen Terry was "created a Dame."[15]

Irving himself was married to Florence O'Callahan with whom he had two sons, and who evidently considered his acting career to be folly. Farson tells the story that, after attending an early performance of his, Florence asked Irving as they were returning home if he intended "to make a fool of [himself] like this all [his] life?" whereupon Irving got out of the carriage and walked away from her and the marriage. Irving supported her and his two sons—Henry Brodribb (Irving's own name) born in 1870, and Laurence, born in 1871—as well as sent her opening night tickets for the rest of his life. It was Stoker, however, who looked after the boys, visiting them at school and supplementing their allowances.

As acting manager of the Lyceum, Stoker closely supervised a staff of one hundred and twenty-eight. He conducted rigorous inspections each opening night before the doors of the theater were unlocked. In charge of finances, he created a bookkeeping system which insured that only he and Irving knew the exact cash flow. His authority is perhaps best illustrated anecdotally; on one occasion, the most dreaded event in the life of a theater occurred when a drapery caught fire. While it was quickly extinguished, one young man ran up the aisle in panic. "[Bram] caught him by the throat and hurled him back on the ground. . . . 'Go back to your seat sir!' [he] said sternly. 'It is cowards like you who cause death to helpless women' " (*PR*, 2:274). Though the story sounds invented, readers of Stoker's fiction have no trouble imagining him speaking in this fashion.

Stoker's dramatic presence, indeed heroism, is marked by a related story. In September of 1882, Stoker observed a man jump overboard from the Thames steamer on which they were both traveling. Stoker jumped in to rescue the man who put up a struggle, though Stoker finally dragged him back to the steamer and carried him home for medical attention. Although the man could not be saved, Stoker was awarded the Bronze Medal of the Royal Humane Society as well as several paragraphs in all the papers. As we shall see, the dramatic rescue becomes a recurrent motif in the fiction.

The story is told that Florence was not happy till they moved from 27 Cheyne Walk where she had confronted the corpse of this suicide in her dining room. Farson speculates that Florence also was increasingly dissatisfied with the time Bram was spending with Irving during these years.[16] She could not have been much happier when, in October of 1883, Stoker took off for America with Irving's company, "the first time an entire theatrical management, with all its equipment, had been brought to America."[17] Stoker's responsibilities were heroic, ranging from planning the entire tour, to arranging tickets and hotel accommodations, to overseeing transportation of all materials for mounting nine plays, to dealing with reporters and company members alike.

The American tours began on the same triumphant note which they were to sound almost yearly for twenty-one years until 25 March 1904; the American people had heard enough about Henry Irving and the Lyceum and the forty or so players of Irving's company managed by Stoker to obviate the need for extensive publicity. In Stoker's words, "Go where [Irving] would, from Maine to Louisiana, from the Eastern to the Western Sea, there was always the same story of loving greeting; of appreciative and encouraging understanding; of heartfelt *au revoirs*, in which gratitude had no little part" (*PR*, 1:288).

During these years Stoker formed his friendships with Whitman and with Mark Twain and came to love America, an affection evident in character portrayals in several of the novels. Moreover, he began to study its society and people, reading everything that came in his way, from the Constitution to etiquette manuals, and speaking to Americans of all occupations.[18] The sense of the country he thus gained was shared in a lecture he delivered at the Birkbeck Institution in London in December 1885 and published as a pamphlet entitled "A Glimpse of America" in 1886. The pamphlet was quite successful; H. M. Stanley, the explorer, told Irving that Stoker "had mistaken [his] vocation— that [he] should be a literary man!" (*PR*, 1:369). Stoker was later informed that Stanley had taken the pamphlet with him to read during his travels in Africa.

In 1887 Stoker returned to the United States to arrange for a tour of the expensive and elaborate Lyceum production of *Faust*. During the tour Stoker was joined by Florence who had determined to brave the Atlantic despite having undergone a shipwreck in the English channel just several months before. But the crossing was too much for her and she never tried it again.

Stoker does not remark on this part of the 1887 tour, but he does describe his last visit with Whitman at this time and records that the poet presented him with a signed 1887 edition of *Leaves of Grass*. This last meeting of the two friends marked the end of what Stoker considered a twenty-year friendship. Clearly this relationship was important to him: his description of it comprises the longest statement about himself in the *Personal Reminiscences*. In this section, Stoker includes a facsimile of a 6 March 1876 letter to him from Whitman and a description of one of his visits to Whitman written by a Thomas Donaldson. Stoker was proud of the description and quotes it, saying, "I think it justifies itself and bears out all that I have already said [about Whitman's fondness for him]." In it Donaldson reports Whitman speaking of Stoker this way: "Well, well; what a broth of a boy he is! My gracious he knows enough for four or five ordinary men; and what tact! Henry Irving knows a good thing when he sees it, eh? Stoker is an adroit lad, and many think that he made Mr. Irving's path, in a business way, a smooth one over here. . . . See that he comes over again to see me before he leaves the country. He's like a breath of good, healthy, breezy sea air" (*PR*, 2:105).

As if Bram did not have enough labor for several during these years, he began to study for the bar as soon as he returned to London, evidently in an effort to fulfill a wish of his father's. In fact, Stoker had functioned as a solicitor, albeit informally, before, drafting rules and bylaws for a variety of organizations,[19] as well as writing his rule book for the clerks of the Petty Sessions. In addition, the 1888 theater season was extraordinarily busy at the Lyceum, with the usual production arrangements running through the night, the enormous volume of correspondence, and the opening and closing night suppers for 300 to 600 guests. Nevertheless, Stoker had managed also to write his first full-length novel: *The Snake's Pass* was published to widespread acclaim in 1890 after running as a serial in several magazines and papers the year before. Moreover, Stoker received some recognition from the literary establishment when "he took his place with other Sampson Low authors at a banquet given in June, 1890 to celebrate the publication of H. M. Stanley's *In Darkest Africa*."[20]

It is likely that Stoker began work on *Dracula* while savoring the success of *The Snake's Pass*. His manuscripts and notes give us a clearer idea of the working out of *Dracula* than we can find elsewhere or than we have for the other works. Ludlam and Farson argue that Stoker was inspired both by a dream (consequent perhaps upon eating dressed crab) and by the tales of one Professor Arminius Vambery, a distinguished professor of Oriental languages at the University of Budapest whom Stoker met on 30 April 1890. However, the *Personal Reminiscences* does not indicate the details of the discussion between Vambery and Stoker,[21] and the notes, now at the Philip H. and A. S. W. Rosenbach Foundation in Philadelphia, indicate that as early as 8 March 1890, Stoker had the novel outlined in its epistolary form, though without the explicit vampirism or the final names and places.

In August of 1890, Stoker took a holiday at Whitby, a coastal town since made famous by *Dracula*. As Joseph S. Bierman observes,[22] sections of Stoker's notes made during that holiday appear verbatim in chapters 6 and 7 of *Dracula* (first in notes dated February 1892). Indeed, Bierman argues, it was at Whitby that Stoker first heard of the historical Dracula, taking notes from a Whitby library book by William Wilkinson, late consul of Bucharest.[23] Stoker followed up his research by reading "Transylvanian Superstitions" by Mme. E. de Laszowska Gerard "which appeared in the July 1885 *Nineteenth Century* magazine . . . then edited by Stoker's acquaintance, Sir James Knowles."[24] Indeed, all of the Stoker materials at the Rosenbach indicate that *Dracula* was scrupulously planned, researched, and revised before its publication in 1897.

The extensiveness of his work on *Dracula* and the numerous other activities in which he was engaged in these years account fully for the unusual length of time Stoker spent on this novel. For example, not until 1892 did Stoker again claim time away from Lyceum business for a holiday and more of his own writing. On his return to London, he was once more immersed in Lyceum obligations, visiting Tennyson, who was very ill and soon to die, to suggest cuts in his *Becket*, the third of the laureate's works which Irving mounted. Tennyson and Stoker got on splendidly (*PR*, 1:201–2), the poet recounting old tales, Stoker helping to reassure the old man of his worth in the eyes of the English people by quoting from memory whole passages of poetry to their author. Before *Becket* opened, Irving mounted *King Lear* but became ill with the flu during the run. Stoker kept the theater open and coerced one of the other actors, W. J. Holloway, to read Lear so the show could go on. Holloway could not help but succeed, according to Stoker, given the support of the rest of the cast and the Lyceum audience, support Stoker himself felt to be essential to all their efforts and for which he was deeply grateful.[25]

In 1893, Stoker took a holiday again, this time to the east coast of Scotland where he discovered the seaport and quaint village at Cruden Bay, site of several stories to come. The refreshment afforded by the holiday was essential for the exertions facing Stoker: a scheduled tour of both the United States and Canada which would include the greatest number of cities and performances yet, a necessity resulting from the financial losses of the previous season.

By the time of the 1895 tour Irving had been knighted—as had Stoker's brother William Thornley. The tour was additionally pleasurable this year because Stoker met with Theodore Roosevelt, then New York City police commissioner. Stoker reports that he wrote in his diary that Roosevelt would someday be president (*PR*, 2:236).

Returning to England in 1896, Stoker continued work on *Dracula*. In November, the Lyceum Company celebrated the twenty-fifth anniversary of Irving's production of *The Bells*, presenting Irving with a two-foot-high bell on which was inscribed the legend written by Stoker: "Honour to Irving. Through the love of his comrades. I ring through the ages" (*PR*, 1:153). Ironically, Stoker was completing the one work which was eventually to make his name at the same time that Henry Irving's long and brilliant career began to falter. A month after the anniversary celebration, Irving staged a successful revival of *Richard III*. After the opening night buffet for five hundred guests, Irving continued his celebrations at a club. Returning home in the early hours of the morning, he apparently tripped on his stairway, causing a rather serious injury to his leg.[26] Incapacitated for ten weeks, Irving suffered also from rumors that the fall was due to drunkenness. Stoker observes reticiently, "in his own rooms that night he met with an accident which prevented his working for ten weeks" (*PR*, 1:126). Whatever the case, more crucial was, first, the loss of more than £6,000, and then the tragic fact that this was what Stoker calls the "turn of the tide": "The disaster of that morning was the beginning of many which struck, and struck, and struck again as though to even up his long prosperity to the normal measure allotted to mankind" (*PR*, 2:325).

From this point on, Irving's fortunes never really recovered. Early in 1898, the Lyceum Company suffered an enormous material loss when the storage building at Bear Lane, Southwark, burned. Stoker arrived to find firemen able only to contain the fire, losses from which included the properties and scenes from forty-four productions; over 2,000 pieces of scenery were destroyed, property totaling in excess of £30,000. Ironically, and tragically, Irving had recently had Stoker reduce the insurance on this property from £10,000 to £6,000. Apparently Irving left to Stoker the job of coping with the enormous difficulties occasioned by the fire, trying to make up for the lost scenes and props, and attempting to assure London that the Lyceum could weather the loss. The quality of his fiction seems to have suffered as a result of the pressures of working for Irving, because *Miss Betty*, published in 1898, is a short and lightweight novel suffering from lack of consideration and revision, among other things.

However, Stoker had a far more serious concern in October 1899 when, on tour in Glasgow, Irving's failing health incapacitated him. He was diagnosed as having pneumonia and pleurisy and required bed rest for nearly two months. During this time, Bram continued to run the tour so that the rest of the actors could support themselves and their families.

According to Ellen Terry's analysis of these days, Irving was at the lowest point in his life, never having been ill before and having to face the recent financial losses. Stoker also attributes his sudden and radical change of plans to depression about ill-health (*PR*, 2:342). Ignoring Stoker's advice, and failing to share his plans with the man who had been his loyal and dedicated aide for over twenty years, Irving signed a tentative agreement with a syndicate to take over the Lyceum. Although Bram must have felt betrayed, as Farson observes, he did what he could to make the best of the deal for Irving. Believing that had Irving followed his advice, at the end of five years he would have had both the theater and the profit promised by the syndicate, Stoker nevertheless negotiated with the syndicate for Irving. He accomplished only two of his goals: Irving would receive a higher salary and would not be required to add his name to the list of directors of the company, an omission which would save Irving's reputation when the syndicate failed.

Once these negotiations were completed, and despite a slight illness of his own, Stoker left to set up the next American tour, coming through the greatest storm in the North Atlantic ever recorded. When he returned to London, however, he found that Irving had signed a contract giving the syndicate rights to and control of all his productions, thus forfeiting what remained of his autonomy and, of course, finally undercutting Stoker's responsibility.[27]

Clearly this was part of a total withdrawal on Irving's part from engagement in any practical affairs, Stoker then having to assume an even greater burden for the daily maintenance of the theater which no longer belonged to them, a task which resulted in his own bout with pneumonia. Although Stoker was hardly recovered when the planned American tour opened, he suffered no diminution of energy, beginning to write *The Mystery of the Sea*, a novel completed during the annual tour of the Irish and English provinces. At the same time, he also wrote a review for *Cosmopolitan Magazine* called "The Art of Ellen Terry." Also during a tour of the provinces, Bram got word that his mother had died peacefully in Dublin at the age of eighty-three.

Stoker returned to America with Irving in the fall of 1901, tour following tour in an attempt to regain solvency. However, the subsequent return to the Lyceum was the last for Irving, the syndicate suffering insurmountable losses as a result of other interests. Though the Irving company went out with a bang not a whimper in the form of an immense coronation party, organized by Bram for King Edward VII, the Lyceum closed its doors in July of 1902. For a well-earned vacation, Stoker returned to Cruden Bay and wrote a good part of a new novel, *The Jewel of Seven Stars*. At the same time, *The Mystery of the Sea* was being published.

Plans for continued work with Irving included a tour of the provinces for the winter of 1901–2 and a return to London with Irving's elaborate *Dante* to be performed at the Theatre Royal in Drury Lane, a play which Irving had arranged to purchase by circumventing Stoker who usually took care of such business. In Stoker's words, Irving "could be very secretive when he wished" (*PR*, 1:272).

In fact, the tour of the provinces marked the end of an era, Ellen Terry leaving the company shortly thereafter, after twenty years of partnership with Irving and Irving mounting his expensive production of *Dante* which, although it managed to run an entire season, occasioned a considerable loss.

When the shareholders in the ruined Lyceum syndicate met to determine their next move, Stoker met with them to defend Irving, pointing out that during the years of his association with the syndicate, Irving had brought in receipts of £29,000. Loyally, Stoker reports "I honestly believe that there was not one person in the room who was not genuinely and heartily glad to be reassured from such an authoritative source as myself as to Irving's position with regard to the Company" (*PR*, 2:318).

Stoker himself came under attack for failing adequately to handle the company's finances. However, most of the evidence indicates that he was not at all to blame for Irving's failure to save and to be judicious. Indeed, a man named Henry Labouchère who had in 1878 offered to back Irving, maintained, "Had it not been for his old friend Bram Stoker, Irving would have been eaten out of home and theatre very speedily."[28] Stoker firmly clears himself of any responsibility for the failure: "I should like to say, on my own account, and for my own protection, inasmuch as I was Sir Henry Irving's business manager, that from first to last I had absolutely no act or part in the formation of the Lyceum Theatre Company [the syndicate]—in its promotion, flotation, or working" (*PR*, 2:319).

Irving's financial situation did not improve through his insistence on taking *Dante* to America. In fact, after disappointments in several cities, Irving and Stoker set the play aside permanently, giving the scenery away at the end of the tour. This change of plans foreshadowed a more major change: this was to be Irving's last American tour. Returning to England Irving announced that he would retire two years later on the fiftieth anniversary of his partnership with theater. After this announcement there were several provincial tours and an excellent run at the Theatre Royal on the last night of which—10 June 1905—Irving triumphed in *Louis XI*, but his career was virtually over. After setting out, apparently in strength, for a farewell provincial tour, Irving became exhausted by the third night. Stoker had little trouble talking him into removing the strenuous *The Bells* from the list of performances, ominously little trouble in Stoker's experience. Stoker indicates he remarked to Loveday: "He acquiesced too easily; I never knew him so meek before. I don't like it" (*PR*, 2:355). The same night Henry Irving collapsed and died at the Midland Hotel in Bradford. Stoker had been summoned and arrived in time only to close his friend's eyes. Stoker recalled that, as they separated earlier in the evening, Irving behaved unusually toward him, shaking his hand warmly: "when men meet every day and every night, handshaking is not part of the routine of friendly life. As I went out he said to me: 'Muffle up your throat, old chap. It's bitterly cold tonight and you have a cold. Take care of yourself! Goodnight, God bless you' " (*PR*, 2:357).

Ludlam believes that this blow was the catalyst to all the anxiety, labor, and strain of the past few years of Stoker's life, causing a stroke which left him weakened and exhausted for weeks. While he recuperated, Stoker watched as many tried to mark, even to capitalize on, the death of the great actor. A variety of books and articles appeared, convincing Stoker that he should offer the public his very privileged glimpses of Henry Irving. So in 1905-6, during which time *The Man* was published, Stoker was working on, not a biography, but a collection of memories to be called *Personal Reminiscences of Henry Irving*. Focusing throughout on Henry Irving the artist, for to Stoker the man was the artist, the *Personal Reminiscences* sustains the tone of deeply affectionate respect and unqualified admiration which marked Stoker's feelings for the man he served so devotedly, one whom Stoker described as "a living embodiment of that fine principle, 'Whatsoever thy hand findeth to do, do it with all thy might.'" (*PR*, 2:339). Clearly, Henry Irving was the most important model in Stoker's life.

Stoker lived only six years beyond Henry Irving, six years which were very different from the glamorous days of suppers and tête-à-têtes with the great painters, composers, literati, kings, queens, and presidents of the day. Returning to London in 1906 from another Cruden Bay working holiday, Stoker was offered his old job as acting manager for a musical rendition of *The Vicar of Wakefield*. Although the play did not succeed and Stoker never returned to the theater again, he continued writing both fiction and articles (the latter, for example, on the popular notion of building a national theater, on Americans as actors, on the theater and art collections of W. S. Gilbert, on censorship); in 1908 he published the novel *Lady Athlyne*. Writing now as much to make money as to fulfill inspiration, Ludlam implies, Stoker was working on two more books during the year: *The Lady of the Shroud*, a *Dracula*-like tale, and the nonfictional study *Famous Imposters*. Although sales of his novels were up, Stoker was working increasingly slowly: "his writing was slower and interrupted by bouts of illness; a niggling frustrating illness that he was unable to throw off. Finally, his gout turned to Bright's disease, and a long and distressing course down hill had begun."[29]

While he was still able to work, and in 1910 he was in Cruden Bay again writing *The Lair of the White Worm*, his life was otherwise constricting. With the marriage of their son Noel, Bram and Florence Stoker moved to a smaller house and Bram discarded books he had spent his early life collecting, "books varying from Kipling, Mark Twain and Stevenson to volumes on Egyptology, a history of the Ku Klux Klan and sets of ordinance maps for the whole of the British Isles."[30] He continued work on the *Lair* into 1912, but on 12 April, he succumbed to what had become an extremely painful illness.

Ludlam's language regarding this illness is interesting, in light of subsequent revelations. He remarks, "Florence's trial as her husband's illness worsened was known only to intimates, as was the extent of Bram's own suffering and incapacity."[31] As Ludlam has recounted the progress of the ailment, not only did Stoker's frame weaken and his energy drain away, but his vision failed progressively.

Ludlam's reticence here may have been an additional goad to Daniel Farson who "felt there was something peculiar about Bram's last years, as if a piece was missing." The puzzle was completed for Farson when he received Stoker's death certificate. Not only, he claims, does it indicate exhaustion as a cause of death, but the "medical terminology on his death certificate reads in full: 'Locomotor Ataxy 6 months Granular Contracted Kidney. Exhaustion. Certified by James Browne M.D.' " Farson checked with a doctor who "was astonished that Dr. Browne had not used a customary subterfuge, such as 'specific disease.' 'Locomotor ataxia' is the equivalent of Tabes Dorsalis and General Paresis, better known as BPI—General Paralysis of the Insane."[32]

In revealing this information, Farson intends, he says, to clarify much that was obscure and speculates that Stoker's "wife's frigidity drove him to other women, probably prostitutes among them; [that] Bram's writing showed signs of guilt and sexual frustration . . . ; [that] he probably caught syphilis around the turn of the century, possibly as early as the year of *Dracula*, 1897."[33] As Farson figures it, Stoker had been forced into celibacy by Florence when Noel was born, a celibacy which Farson believes lasted for twenty years until Stoker rebelled. It is not my intention to deal with these claims. Presumably one cannot argue the existence of the death certificate as Farson describes it. One may observe, however, that Farson seems to have inferred, from rather scant evidence, intimate interactions of a marriage he never witnessed. So it is perhaps best to conclude that he is conjecturing regarding that marriage.

Moreover, the final words on Bram Stoker's life should not be these. All evidence indicates that he was a cultivated and dedicated, if rather self-important, man who was admired by hundreds of people whom his life touched: artists, rulers, and the audience in the pit alike. His life is in some ways best reflected by the *Personal Reminiscences* whose ambiguous title refers to its author as well as to its subject. If there is a strain of the bizarre running through his life, and I believe there is, we need to provide a more cautious and thoughtfully considered examination of his writings than has been undertaken so far in order at least to demonstrate it if not to account for it. "In literary biography the material which must guide us is the writer's work. . . . We start, in other words, with the achievement,"[34] cautiously searching for "the figure under the carpet, the evidence in the reverse of the tapestry, the life-myth of a given mask."[35]

## Chapter Two
# The Romances

All of Stoker's novels are romances in the sense that all depict the forming of couples, the conflicts and misunderstandings between partners (or, in the cases of the horror tales, problems occasioned by the forces of evil), and the overcoming of difficulties in resolutions of happy marriages. These are novels of sentiment in the eighteenth-century tradition, novels whose heroines are divinely beautiful and, frequently, fabulously wealthy, whose heroes are broad of shoulder, noble of face and bearing, and Olympian in strength. Heroines require rescue from compromising situations, or from the sea, a bog, or a vampire; heroes learn to understand the true nature of Woman. On the whole, with one striking exception, *The Man*, the pure romances are far less interesting than the tales of horror, those novels which include mystery and the preternatural and which employ the Gothic components of horror and the uncanny.

The present discussion of the romances covers three of the four major works written by Stoker in that genre, and describes their major attributes. The distinction between the fictional works discussed in this chapter and those examined in later chapters is not that the tales of horror do not include romance plots but that their major and characteristic effects and achievements result from the subordination and incorporation of the romance plots into the suspense and general uncanniness of the Gothic genre. The novels which are primarily romances—*The Snake's Pass* (1890), *Miss Betty* (1898), and *The Man* (1905)—which are discussed here, and *Lady Athlyne* (1908), which is not, while far weaker are nonetheless important in terms of Stoker's corpus. Indeed, all demonstrate the major thematic characteristics marking Stoker's fiction: the ambivalence toward woman, the typical Oedipal configuration of character relationships, the blurring or confusion of identities, and the recurrent rescue motifs. The plot of *Lady Athlyne* is based almost exclusively on a case of falsified identity which is condoned and resolved at the end of the novel through the romance of the two protagonists whom we last see locked in a triangular embrace including the heroine's father, an awkward image of which unfortunately Stoker was especially fond. The three novels discussed here include the same components.

## The Snake's Pass

Written in the late 1880s and first published in 1890 (with a "new and cheaper edition" appearing in 1909),[1] *The Snake's Pass* is Stoker's first full-length novel. In it, Stoker both employs a conventional romance pattern in which hero meets girl, hero loses girl, hero finds girl and treasure, and foreshadows the tales of mystery and horror to come. Moreover, *The Snake's Pass* demonstrates Stoker's talents for building suspense and for researching folklore and scientific theory alike.

Set on the west coast of Ireland, *The Snake's Pass* is narrated by its hero, Arthur Severn, a young man who has recently inherited considerable wealth from a great aunt who had provided him from the time of his parents' deaths a rather stern and unimaginative private education with a tutor. Just returned from the grand tour of Europe, Arthur is traveling to visit friends when he journeys through a part of Ireland which arouses his curiosity and compels his imagination. At first Arthur is struck by the beauty of the coastal landscape:

Between two great mountains of grey and green, as the rock cropped out between the tufts of emerald verdure, the valley, narrow as a gorge, ran due west towards the sea. There was just room for the roadway, half cut in the rock, beside the narrow strip of dark lake of seemingly unfathomable depth that lay far below between perpendicular walls of frowning rock. As the valley opened, the land dipped steeply, and the lake became a foam-fringed torrent, widening out into pools and miniature lakes as it reached the lower ground. In the wide terrace-like steps of the shelving mountain there were occasional glimpses of civilization emerging from the almost primal desolation which immediately surrounded us—clumps of trees, cottages, and the irregular outlines of stonewalled fields, with black stacks of turf for winter firing piled here and there. Far beyond was the sea—the great Atlantic—with a wildly irregular coast-line studded with a myriad of clustering rocky islands. (*SP*, 1–2)

This lovely scene is almost immediately blotted out by a violent storm which forces Arthur and his driver, Andy Sullivan—along with a number of local characters—to take refuge at a hospitable "sheebeen," a cottage owned by the widow Kelligan. There, during a cozy and companionable meal of steamed potatoes and pieces of herring, Arthur hears the local legends of the Snake's Pass, "shleenanaher," and the Hill of the Lost Golden Crown, "Knockcalltecrore," a degenerate form of the original "Knock-no-callte-croin-oir" we are later told (*SP*, 30). The stories explaining these names are two, one mythic, one naturalistic. The former derives from the legends surrounding St. Patrick's ridding Ireland of its snakes. When St. Patrick was driving the snakes into the sea, many went to their king for aid, but St. Patrick followed them and drove them to their deaths. Then St. Patrick had to deal with the king of the snakes who refused to follow the order into the sea, claiming he was on his own land. St. Patrick himself claimed the land, but the king of the snakes said he would refuse to recognize the claim until the saint found his golden crown. With this, the snake dove down into his lake and through the base of Knockcalltecrore—draining the lake and hiding the crown on his way—and slid out to sea, "dhrivin' through the rock an' makin' the clift that they call the Shleenanaher—an' that's Irish for the Shnake's Pass . . ." (*SP*, 22).

The second explanation attributes the name of Knockcalltecrore to the story that, during a French invasion of Ireland, the French brought an enormous amount of gold to bribe the locals into aiding them against the English. This gold, carried in an iron chest, was taken by several of the French soldiers through the area and onto Knockcalltecrore but, according to the late father of Bat Moynahan who tells the story, the men, horses, and chest all disappeared, presumably into the shifting bog which plagues the local residents.

Fascinated by the stories, Arthur feels a rather mystical as well as mysterious connection to the area and is eager to hear more. Fortunately, he does not have long to wait as Stoker introduces almost all the rest of the characters immediately. The west side of Knockcalltecrore is owned by two men, Phelim Joyce and the villain Murtagh Murdock, called by the locals Black Murdock, the Gombeen Man or usurer. Murdock has been eager to get his hands on Joyce's property, so he can continue his search for the lost gold. The men argue violently in the cottage and Joyce strikes Murdock across the face with his riding whip, leaving a "livid scar." The local priest, who also has been part of the company gathered at Mrs. Kelligan's, warns Murdock that "as he reaps so he shall sow" and comforts Joyce with the thought that frequently our apparent ills turn out to be part of a benevolent divine plan. The plot of *The Snake's Pass* is now set to work itself out according to the priest's predictions, with the addition of one further element. This last component appears first in the form of an enchanting, if disembodied, voice Arthur hears when he and Andy drive Joyce home. The voice belongs to Joyce's daughter, Norah, who is waiting for her father outside their house, but whom Arthur cannot see for the darkness of the night.

Continuing on his travels to visit his friends, Arthur cannot forget either Norah's voice or the legends of Knockcalltecrore and, within six weeks, he returns to the region, determined to know more. On his return, he finds that the Joyces have moved into Murdock's house, as Murdock has taken over their property and continued his search for the lost gold, now with the aid of an engineer, Dick Sutherland. Dick, it turns out, is an old school chum of Arthur's, and is working for the Gombeen Man only because he had signed a contract, having subsequently seen enough of Murdock to loathe him. Stoker's research is evident as Dick explains to Arthur both that little has been written about shifting bogs and that he has a theory—which he describes in detail—concerning those on the west side of Knockcalltecrore.

Aware both of Dick's interest in bogs and Arthur's in Norah, Andy Sullivan drives them over to the site of another bog at Knocknacar, a hill where, unknown to Arthur, Norah Joyce is known to walk. Both men find what they seek, and Dick arranges to try to drain this bog as an experiment to test his theories and to enable him better to predict what will happen at Knockcalltecrore. Art, in his turn, comes upon a beautiful young woman with whom he immediately falls in love, forgetting Norah Joyce. Seeing her several days in a row, Arthur becomes certain that she likes him as well though she does not mention her name. He is, however, thoroughly exasperated with Andy who keeps teasing him about going to see Norah. The reader, in turn, is rather exasperated with Arthur for not realizing that the woman he loves and Norah are the same. But Arthur's obtuseness is essential for Stoker to develop a rivalry between Arthur and Dick for, while the former has fallen in love with Norah at Knocknacar, the latter has fallen in love with her at Knockcalltecrore. Not able to be in two places at one time, Norah is seen by only one man at a time, leading to a discussion between the friends of their alternating fortunes. Only when Art meets Norah near Knockcalltecrore, after looking unsuccessfully for her for a number of days at Knocknacar, does he find out from her who she is. Despite what Dick has told him, he proposes immediately and makes certain he will not see Dick again until he has been accepted—an event which occurs the next day. Indeed, his first thought of Dick was the fear that Dick might have proposed to Norah first. However, when he confronts Dick with his success, Arthur is able to prove that he had never intended the rivalry, by giving Dick what was to have been a wedding present for him and Norah: the deed to Joyce's former property, land which Art had purchased from Murdock, leaving the latter a month in which to find the treasure before the sale would be completed. With this proof, Dick is convinced of his friend's loyalty and the scene ends happily: "Having torn the paper across he put his arm over my shoulder as he used to do when we were boys . . ." (*SP*, 194).

The two stories of the novel, the romance and the mystery of the bog and the lost gold, are even more closely bound up in the last third of *The Snake's Pass*, not only by Andy's teasing of Art about "bogs"—which has come to mean girls, an equation one does not wish to investigate further—but also by the conventional identification of the girl with the treasure, a recurrent motif in Stoker's novels. Following Andy's advice that he hold tight to Joyce, reminding the reader of myths of Proteus, and get a firm answer regarding his marriage to Norah, Art pushes for a date to be set "when he could have her." Joyce responds, " 'When the threasure of Knockcalltecrore is found, thin ye may claim her if ye will, an' I'll freely let her go!' As he spoke, there came before my mind the strong idea that we were all in the power of the Hill— that it held us . . ." (*SP*, 207–8).

All this while Murdock, greed incarnate, has been working frantically to find the treasure of gold, using magnets and grappling hooks, going over the land inch by inch, and buying the aid of Bat Moynahan by keeping him drunk. He is, moreover, damming up the stream at the top of the land and digging into the clay banks at the bottom, thereby endangering everyone by increasing the chances that the bog will shift. Dick warns him of this repeatedly, especially pointing out the vulnerability of the house he is now living in, the one he took from the Joyces. They, however, seem safe, since Murdock had built his house on a ledge of rock. Nevertheless, as the suspense increases, and the rain continues to pour down, Arthur has a series of terrifying nightmares:

I seemed to live over again in isolated moments all the past weeks; but in such a way that the legends and myths and stories of Knock-calltecrore which I had heard were embodied in each moment. Thus, Murdock had always a part in the gloomy scenes, and got inextricably mixed up with the King of the Snakes. They freely exchanged personalities, and at one time I could see the Gombeen Man defying St. Patrick, whilst at another the Serpent seemed to be struggling with Joyce, and, after twisting round the mountain, being only beaten off by a mighty blow from Norah's father, rushing to the sea through the Shleenanaher. (*SP*, 261–62)

The night before Norah is to leave for Paris to pursue a lady's education for two years in order better to fit herself to be the wife of a gentleman, Art's dreams and fears are so compelling that he and Dick and Andy set off at one in the morning in the torrential rain to assure themselves of the Joyces' safety. Art's fears are too fully realized when they learn from Norah's aunt that Norah had set out earlier that night to find her father who had not returned home. The danger seems even greater when they learn that earlier in the evening Murdock had poisoned Norah's guard dog and tried unsuccessfully to lure her to his cabin. The men separate the better to find Norah and Joyce. Arthur finally hears Norah calling for help and is in time to rescue her from Murdock's clutches but, after he places her on a rock and then goes to get water to revive her, the bog shifts and he becomes caught: "But even as I stood there—and I had not delayed an unnecessary second—the ground under me seemed to be giving way. There was a strange shudder or shiver below me, and my feet began to sink" (*SP*, 330). Only Norah's recovery at his crying out and her strong hands are able to save him as she pulls him onto the rock with her.

Murdock, however, is not fated to be so lucky. When Art arrived to rescue Norah, Murdock ran for his house. But as the bog began to shift, "he had evidently felt some kind of shock or change, for he came out of the house full of terror. For an instant he seemed paralyzed with fright as he saw what was happening. And it was little wonder! For in that instant the whole house began to sink into the earth—to sink as a ship founders in a stormy sea, but without the violence and turmoil that marks such a catastrophe. There was something more terrible—more deadly in that silent, causeless destruction than in the devastation of the earthquake or the hurricane" (*SP*, 334). When Norah and Arthur discover that Joyce is quite safe, the story is essentially over since, as the priest predicted, Murdock reaped as he sowed, and Joyce was ultimately saved by what seemed earlier to be his greatest misfortune.

Stoker concludes the novel in a summary fashion as, after daybreak, the Joyces and Art and Dick discover both the treasure chest and a cave in which Norah locates the lost crown of the king of the snakes. More valuable, the cave reveals the presence of limestone so, for the next two years while Norah is in Paris, Dick is able to make Knockcalltecrore, now entirely owned by Arthur, the utopian home he envisioned.

*The Snake's Pass* indicates the direction of most of Stoker's fiction to follow. The primary focus and achievement is the creation of a suspenseful tale, frequently turning on mysteries and/or legends, and punctuated with vivid, often frightening, description. Again typically, the romance is highly conventionalized and the heroine idealized out of all believability. Indeed, as was indicated in the reference to Proteus, the romance in Stoker's fiction is characteristically a version of the mythic quest story in which the hero wins his manhood, the treasure, and the princess at the end of a series of trials and adventures. In the very first pages of *The Snake's Pass,* Arthur claims he feels alive and conscious for the first time in his life: "I felt exalted in a strange way, and impressed at the same time with a new sense of the reality of things. It almost seemed as if through that opening valley, with the mighty Atlantic beyond and the piling up of the storm-clouds overhead, I passed into a new and more real life" (*SP,* 4).

Moreover, the romance in Stoker always manifests elements of the Oedipal situation, entailing rivalries between siblings or father figures and sons and revealing a maternal figure underlying the character of the heroine. In *The Snake's Pass,* the elements suggestive of the Oedipal triangle are both relatively obvious and rather ingeniously interwoven between the current story and characters and the legend of Shleenanaher and Knockcalltecrore. The antagonism between father and son is sufficiently sublimated so as not to be readily apparent in the relationship of Joyce and Arthur, although we should recall Andy's advice to Art to hold tight to Joyce in order to secure Norah. The only explicit rendering of conflict between these two occurs when Norah calls out to be saved from Black Murdock and Arthur is gratified to observe, even at such a moment, that she calls for him before she cries out for her father.

What is much more apparent, of course, is the antagonism between all the men and Black Murdock—a constellation repeated in *Dracula*—who, Satan-like, curses and defies God, the Trinity, and anyone else who might get in his way. Murdock and Joyce are paired as primary antagonists, and seem to be about the same age, but part of Murdock's plotting includes a proposal to Norah, obviously to get his hands on land she owns, as well as vague threats to her reputation. Indeed, at one point we hear of a foul rumor concerning her which we are to assume originated with the Gombeen Man. The infantile level of the battle against Murdock is revealed in the melodramatic dialogue in these scenes, with the Gombeen Man being called a "dastardly soul" and warned: "take care how you cross her path or mine again, or you shall rue it to the last day of your life. Come, Norah, it is not fit that you should contaminate your eyes or your ears with the presence of this wretch!" (*SP,* 248). The hostility toward Black Murdock is rationalized in a variety of ways; first of all, he so clearly deserves it that Joyce, Art, and Dick all feel reasonably justified, even when they strike him—which each does at a different moment—the younger men doing so when he threatens or reviles Norah; second, the hostility is tempered by Dick's repeated warnings to Murdock that he is vulnerable should the bog shift; and, finally, when the inevitable does occur, Norah and Art shout warnings at him from the safety of their rock.

Despite these rationalizations, there can be no doubt that Black Murdock is the archetypal villain, Dracula's precursor, both Satan whose divine counterpart is God, and the king of the snakes whose foil is St. Patrick. Thus, *The Snake's Pass* entails at least two sets of doubling: doubling by splitting of one paternal figure into the good father—Joyce—and the bad—Murdock; and doubling by multiplying, doubling Joyce with St. Patrick and Murdock with the king of the snakes. This latter occurs, as we have seen, in Art's nightmare in which Murdock is "mixed up with the King of the

Snakes . . . and at one time I could see the Gombeen Man defying St. Patrick, whilst at another the serpent seemed to be struggling with Joyce . . ." (*SP*, 261–62). Additional doubling occurs in the sibling rivalry between Dick and Art, a rivalry which is more conventional and acceptable, and therefore more explicit, than that between the son and the father.

This constellation of figures and series of actions recurs in Stoker's fiction, most notably in *Dracula*. In both novels, ambivalence toward the father figure is realized by its splitting into good father/bad father, with the young hero, from whose point of view the story is told, realizing both his desire to be protected by the good father and his desire to destroy the bad.

The role of the female is more fully explored, or revealed, in other novels, especially in *The Man* and in *Dracula*, but even here the underlying maternal component is felt in a scene in which Norah cleans up a mussed and dirtied Arthur:

That toilet was to me a sweet experience, and is a sweet remembrance now. It was so wifely in its purpose and its method, that I went through it in a languourous manner—like one in a delicious dream. When, with a blush, she brought me her own brush and comb and began to smooth my hair, I was as happy as it is given to a man to be. There is a peculiar sensitiveness in their hair to some men, and to have it touched by hands that they love is a delicious sensation. When my toilet was complete Norah took me by the hand and made me sit down beside her. (*SP*, 223–24)

All of Stoker's novels entail the winning (and therefore the threat of loss) of a woman's love. Typically, the woman is maternal and saves or is saved by the hero. Intriguingly, Arthur has another nightmare in which he foreshadows Norah's saving him from the bog, but in which dream it is not he but Murdock whom she is saving, reiterating the rivalry with the bad father and suggesting the ambivalence toward the mother. Frequently then, though not always, the hero is involved in a rivalry with another man, a paternal or sibling figure. That this component of the novels does not seem to be the one on which Stoker spent most of his time makes it even more revealing for it is the least elaborate, least revised—as a consequence, least artful—part of his work. It may, therefore, be more revealing biographically, though the very conventionality of the plot militates against too rigorous a pursuit of the biographical. Nevertheless, since Stoker returns repeatedly to this constellation and develops it throughout his work, it is worth observing in detail in his first novel.

According to Stoker's biographer Harry Ludlam, "The press was unanimous in praise of 'The Snake's Pass,'" and Stoker received personal compliments from Tennyson and Gladstone.[2] These accolades indicate the charm of the folklore and characters and, indeed, the scene at Mrs. Kelligan's sheebeen captures both local color and country customs—the rolling of the steamed potatoes in coarse salt is an especially nice touch—and a sense of insularity conducive to the perpetuation of mysterious legends. The scene is described so vividly that, when new characters appear out of the violent storm, the reader can see the steam rising from their clothes. The character of Andy Sullivan is vividly drawn also, providing just the sort of comic relief the plot requires for, without his teasing of Art about "bogs," the romance would be portrayed without the necessary leavening of humor. One of the best scenes depicting the progress of Arthur's love for Norah relies on a brand of self-consciousness and self-mockery which Arthur learns from Andy. Arthur is attempting to appear casual as he makes his very deliberate way up Knocknacar to find Norah:

I loitered awhile here and there on the way up. I diverted my steps now and then as if to make inquiry into some interesting object. I tapped rocks and turned stones over, to the discomfiture of various swollen pale-coloured worms and nests of creeping things. With the end of my stick I dug up plants, and made here and there unmeaning holes in the ground as though I were actuated by some direct purpose known to myself and not understood by others. In fact I acted as a hypocrite in many harmless and unmeaning ways, and rendered myself generally obnoxious to the fauna and flora of Knocknacar. (*SP*, 111).

Through the rest of the story, when Arthur loses this perspective on his behavior, Andy is always there to remind him, and to relieve the reader.

It is true, nevertheless, that, as with the sentimental novels in general, all Stoker's characters tend to be one-dimensional, highly stylized, and romanticized types, and Andy is not much of an exception. Moreover, Stoker's stereotyping reveals an elitism and racism apparent throughout the novels. Frequent and gratuitous references to "niggers" appear here as elsewhere and, while Stoker is clearly fond of utopian schemes by which all the people will benefit, the schemes are not even democratic, let alone socialist, and the people concerned remain a vague abstraction. In *The Snake's Pass,* for instance, though part of Norah's attraction is her natural intelligence, her peasant costume, and her strong, tanned hands with which she is able to save Art, all the characters agree she needs new clothes and schooling to suit her properly to be a gentleman's wife.

In his fiction, then, Stoker writes from within an established social order which he does not question or criticize. His focus and major interest is the working out of a mystery or a complication, one caused by the presence of evil which must be expelled and/or by misunderstanding between lovers. His greatest strengths lie in the creation of suspense and dread, in vivid descriptions of a nature either lushly pastoral or sublimely diabolical. The romance component of the novels is typically weak, comprised of an obvious Oedipal configuration, and, more subtly and significantly, an ambivalence toward the female character. In the early novels this ambivalence is not striking—the heroines in fact suffer from their excessively idealized portrayals—but, with *Dracula* and the subsequent novels, as Stoker focuses increasingly on the nightmarish and preternatural, the portrait of Woman is increasingly negative, indeed even terrifying and, as we shall see, delineates the pre-Oedipal rather than the Oedipal mother. Indeed, the horror and fascination of Stoker's later novels derive from their visions of Woman, visions not yet evident in the early romances.

## Miss Betty

First published in February 1898,[3] on the heels of *Dracula*'s appearance, *Miss Betty* is the weakest of Stoker's romances. Short of novel length and complication, it is a straightforward tale of the faith of a pure—and, of course, beautiful—woman and the regeneration of her miscreant fiancé. Betty Pole, like all Stoker's protagonists, is orphaned at an early age with only maiden aunts, trustees of estates, and faithful servants to guide her. Her own virtue, good sense, and the memory of advice and a special trust fund given her by a great-grandfather enable her to perform not only as a virtuous Victorian woman but to save the soul—and neck—of her fiancé turned outlaw.

Betty Pole meets Rafe Otwell under dramatic circumstances which one would like to consider extraordinary were they not so typical in sentimental fiction. The story proper begins the year after the crowning of King George in the early 1700s on the occasion of a boat race on the Thames. All aristocratic London has turned out, many families in their own boats, the better to view the gallant oarsmen. Miss Betty is no exception, afloat with an Aunt Priscilla, a cousin Hester, and Mrs. Abigail, the faithful retainer who has been with Betty since childhood. As the boats sweep up and down the river, Betty realizes she has attracted "a handsome young fellow with black hair and dark eyes and a proud bearing [who] carried well the elegant dress he wore (*MB*, 31). Mrs. Abigail rightly believes him to be Betty's "true Prince Charming," and conveniently, albeit unintentionally, drops her favorite hat into the water. Betty reaches over to retrieve the hat, and her boat, colliding with another, tips her into the water. Prince Charming, quickest of all the surrounding heroes, jumps in and saves Miss Betty who is brought to shore dripping wet but no less beautiful, still valiantly clutching Mrs. Abigail's hat. Proper introductions are effected quickly and Rafe Otwell becomes a regular guest at the house on Cheyne Walk.

The courtship of Rafe and Betty is handled in a perfunctory fashion, Stoker being far more interested in the complications to follow. The test and failure of Rafe's character turns, not atypically, on his financial situation. Having run through a small inheritance, his only hope is to be favored and subsidized by his distant kinsman, the powerful Sir Robert Walpole, "now the virtual ruler of England, since he controlled both the Treasury and the Exchequer" (*MB*, 51).[4]

Sir Robert has plans of consolidating his power by allying himself to a "great house" through the marriage of his young kinsman, Rafe, to the Lady Mary. This puts Rafe in an exceedingly awkward position, since he has failed to mention to Sir Robert his betrothal to Miss Betty and believes, wrongly we are told, that Sir Robert would oppose the match. Rafe's relationship with Betty, however, is all he could wish and, consequently, his embarrassed circumstances are doubly painful. Running quickly through the funds Sir Robert has advanced him. Rafe is put further at his kinsman's mercy. Lady Mary, old and ugly, is still in need of a husband but Rafe finally admits he is betrothed to another. Sir Robert determines to tighten the screws again by offering just a bit more money to increase Rafe's debts and dependencies. Betty, too, is pressuring Rafe to let her help him: "Always thoughtful, she now became blessed with a sweet gravity—that gravity which so becomes the wife potential, the one whose self is forgotten in the needs of others" (*MB*, 72). Rafe's "masculine pride" cannot allow him to accept money from Betty—though he runs through Sir Robert's loans quickly—so he sees no legal way to survive the two remaining years till Betty's majority and their marriage, when he can get his hands on her money with honor.

Lacking in moral courage, we are reminded, Rafe disappears for days at a time, returning to Betty with expensive gifts, a new swagger, and an uncharacteristic, abrasive laugh. The reader soon learns to link this behavior with the stories of a courageous highway robber who has recently threatened payroll shipments on lonely roads; Betty, too, needs but little time to realize where Rafe has obtained his new wealth and swagger. She concludes that, "unworthy though he had proved, she loved him still; and as even he had given her life to her, so if need be should that life be given for him in return" (*MB*, 95). Under the guise of traveling to her country house at Much Hadam to improve her weakening health, Betty overcomes the objections of her relatives and Mrs. Abigail and effects a complicated plan for the rescue of Rafe from his evil ways. Correctly calculating his next robbery attempt, she makes haste to substitute herself for the courier, whom all of London seems to know will be disguised as a woman, and thereby confronts Rafe in the very act of attempting to rob her. As a consequence of a rather confused scene, Stoker being unsure who is to dominate whom and who is to feel most ashamed, Rafe leaves the country to save his neck (the gibbet has been introduced earlier in the book) and to do penance. Betty gives him the special trust fund her great-grandfather bequeathed her to help someone in just such a situation, bringing the novel back to its opening scenes, and takes her way to Much Hadam to wait for news of her lover, for years if need be.

Five years pass in fact, during which time Betty anonymously repays all his debts and thefts and her cousin Fenton realizes her great acts of faith and love, before Rafe returns, repentant and rich. The resolution occurs as rapidly as the exposition of the novel, and our final view is of Betty clasping hands with her two men, Cousin Fenton and the reclaimed Rafe. "The years that had passed had changed Betty from a girl into a woman, and though her heart and mind retained all their bashfulness, there was a new yielding to the sweet impulses which came to her, as to all the daughters of Eve. . . . When she felt her lover in her arms . . . , she wanted something more than the simple assurance that he would not leave her again" (*MB*, 153–54).

Clearly, the strength of *Miss Betty* does not lie in its simple-minded and moralistic plot. Moreover, characters are differentiated only according to function and introduced only as needed, then dropped. For example, Miss Betty has a brother, Robert, who is on stage only briefly for the sole purpose of foiling Rafe—Robert is also extravagant and takes money from Betty—and inciting him to buy Betty expensive gifts he cannot afford. When through with Robert, Stoker announces, "Henceforth he passes out of the story"

(*MB,* 60). Furthermore, with the single strand plot, Stoker's foreshadowing seems both heavy-handed and mechanical. Just prior to the episode of the hat and Rafe's rescue of Betty early in the novel, for instance, Stoker mentions that "all sorts of mishaps occurred" on the water. In sum, the plot lurches forward in staccato gestures, as does the dialogue which is not well individualized. Stoker was evidently far more interested in the complication of Rafe's profligacy and Betty's salvation of him. The dreariest component is, of course, the sentimentality, especially as it pertains to Stoker's portrayal of the ideal woman. Betty is everything that is good and true and submissive, so much so that even Stoker seems bored: "For if he was poor, she had enough for both, and it would be only an added sweetness to say to him when the time came—if it ever did come—'I give you all I have, Rafe—And yet how little! You gave me your name—a woman has none worth having in our English law; my life is yours already' *and so forth*" (*MB,* 42; my italics).

The novel does contain some good touches, however. Once the plot is well underway, the writing improves somewhat, as does the characterization: Rafe's hard laugh, Betty's genuine concern, and Cousin Fenton's pleasure in being able to cheer Betty—ironically with information which reveals Rafe's doings—are all stronger than other portraits in the novel. The characterization of Mrs. Abigail deepens, too, in her sulking at not being told more than the housemaids of Betty's plans to get to Much Hadam. Typically, too, Stoker is strongest in his description, albeit melodramatic, of natural scenes reflecting a human mood. As Betty takes leave of the Cheyne Walk house and the scenes of Rafe's courtship of her, Stoker narrates: "Here she remained for a long time, standing still as if carved out of stone. The red glare of the sunset fell full upon her, smiting her pale face and snowy garments till from head to foot she looked as if dipped in blood" (*MB,* 100).

Perhaps the best element in *Miss Betty* is the characterization of the unscrupulous Sir Robert who, while rather archetypally villainous, at least walks around a room, considers and reconsiders, moves his hands in calculating ways, and altogether demonstrates an animation equaled only by Betty at her most "unfeminine," riding to forestall Rafe.

Fortunately, *Miss Betty* is the least exciting of Stoker's novels. The text indicates no great degree of forethought or revision and is most interesting to Stoker's readers as a demonstration that Stoker's strengths lie elsewhere than in tales of pure romance.

### The Man

*The Man,* published in 1905,[5] is Stoker's most leisurely and sophisticated romance; indeed, with regard to characterization, it is his most painstaking and satisfying novel. None of his other novels entails the time and detail devoted to the examination of complex motivation as does this one. Moreover, it is also the most direct and lengthy analysis of female sexuality and behavior Stoker undertook and, although his conclusions typify Victorian era confusions and stereotypes as well as Stoker's own ambivalences, the strengths of the female protagonist are given a good deal of liberty. *The Man* is also a bizarre book, playing on a clearly defined question of sexual identity: the female hero is named Stephen Norman after her father who very much desired a son from his only marriage, one made late in his life. Since from the outset Stephen both tries to be her father's son and questions conventional sex roles, the reader assumes that "the Man" refers to Stephen. Stoker is not writing *Orlando,* however; late in the book one discovers that the title refers explicitly to Harold An Wolf, clearly the male protagonist but just as clearly secondary to Stephen in interest and attention paid to him. This rather belated revelation parallels and sets forth the final disposition of sex roles in the novel: while Stoker allows Stephen considerable latitude in her behavioral experimentation when she is a girl and a young woman, she finally learns what it "really" means, according to Stoker, to be a woman. "She was all woman now; all patient, and all submissive. She waited [for] the man; and the man was coming!" When she learns the lesson of womanhood, she also learns the identity of her true love; the reader discovers that Harold is "the Man" and that Stephen Norman is no man.

The plot of *The Man* is not much more complicated than those of the other romances. The major characters include Stephen, her father, Harold An Wolf, another boy Stephen grows up with named Leonard Everard, and Stephen's great-aunt Laetitia Rowly, who raised Stephen's mother and who becomes Stephen's surrogate mother after her own dies in giving birth to Stephen. As is true in many Victorian novels in addition to Stoker's, most characters grow up without mothers, a device allowing the characters to explore behaviors and make mistakes against which their mothers presumably would have warned them. In Stephen's case, the lack of a mother is even more crucial, for Stephen has no model of the proper Victorian wife; no woman Stephen knows is married. Additionally, in the course of the novel, both Stephen and Harold lose their fathers, forcing them into positions both of premature responsibility and of misunderstanding. Stephen's difficulties are very much obviated, more or less in the nick of time, by the assistance first of Aunt Laetitia and then, when she dies, of a strange "Silver Lady" who doubles for the aunt. One of Stoker's typical difficulties is the introduction of gratuitous characters or, viewed another way, the employment of characters about whom we are not told enough to see them function successfully as foils or in a subplot, the Silver Lady being such a character.

As the small number of characters indicates, the plot of *The Man* is clear and unfolds in a single chronological dimension, although the author occasionally returns to an earlier point in time to be able to inform the reader what another character has been doing in the meanwhile. Growing up without a mother and indulged by a father to whom she is a son, Stephen Norman begins to question conventional restrictions on female behavior. Raised, however, both in the lap of luxury and out of society on a large estate in a place called Normanstand, Stephen finds little opportunity to develop "masculine" skills or even to imagine possible behaviors. For example, one of her most gleeful moments as a young girl occurred when her uncle Gilbert put his fez on her head and penciled in a moustache and thickened the eyebrows on her face. As Stephen gets a bit older, however, and even before her father dies, she wishes to assume her role in the country and among "their people" with as much vigor as he. This she does, to the extent at any rate of fulfilling the rather feudal obligations of the lady Victorian aristocrat, visiting and aiding the poor, and so forth. Additionally, much to the dismay of her proper aunt, she expresses a wish to attend the Petty Sessions Court with her father to improve her knowledge of the difficulties and evils of the lives of her people.

Stephen feels, moreover, that she needs further to test her theory that women should be allowed rights and privileges equal to those men enjoy and, consequently, determines to propose marriage to Leonard Everard. The complication of the novel's plot lies in this determination which is, not surprisingly, a hideous mistake. First of all, Leonard is clearly the wrong man; from what we know of him, though Stephen does not, he is an unbounded egotist, caring for no one and nothing but his own pleasure and dominance. Interestingly, in terms of the novel's final stand on proper sex role behavior which stresses the dominance of the man, it is Leonard's desire to dominate which both attracts Stephen and deceives her about him. Further, Leonard is a profligate, deep in debt, and, possibly, responsible for the pregnancy of a young peasant woman less fortunate than Stephen. Finally, Leonard is a coward, a fact demonstrated to the reader on an occasion when Stephen willfully ignores the advice of Harold and, with Leonard, enters the old church crypt where her mother is entombed. Distraught by the discovery of her mother's coffin, Stephen faints away in the darkness of the crypt. Harold arrives just in time to discover the cowardly Leonard rushing out alone into the daylight and fresh air. While Harold rescues Stephen, Leonard hangs around and it is the latter's face Stephen sees first, leading her to the conclusion that he carried her from the crypt. A sensitive, self-effacing sort, Harold does not correct her and neither does the mean and craven Leonard. In consequence, an animosity is born between the men and a misapprehension regarding Leonard is nourished in Stephen's heart. The reader, however, knows that Leonard is not the man; he is far beyond the reclaiming Rafe Otwell enjoys from the good graces of Miss Betty.

Moreover, the reader knows that Harold is the man. From the moment of their first meeting as the children of two close friends, their fathers, Harold and Stephen have loved and trusted each other. Their lives have had meaning by virtue of shared experiences and, when Harold's father dies, neither wishes for anything more than the fulfillment of their childhood dream that Harold would come and live at Normanstand and be Stephen's father's other son. This dream is fulfilled with the effect of strengthening the ties between Stephen and Harold as well as initiating Harold into all the affairs of the Normans. Harold is on the scene of Stephen's father's accident and, before the elder man dies, he entrusts Stephen to Harold, saying it is his dearest hope that Harold and Stephen should someday marry but that Harold should give Stephen time and her own choice. This advice becomes for Harold not only law but both his temporary downfall and his ultimate triumph, for it indicates to him his duty with regard to Stephen. Believing that Stephen is too young for thoughts of marital love, Harold suppresses his desires for her and, indeed, avoids her.

For her part, Stephen is as young as Harold surmises but not too young to try out her theories of woman's equality. Limited by her narrow field of activity, Stephen concludes, not so much that she wishes to *marry* Leonard, whom she has not seen for some time and whose true character she has never gauged, but that she wishes to *propose* to him. Since Harold puts himself "outside practical range" and since Stoker claims that while "a man loves a woman and seeks that woman's love, a woman seeks love" regardless, apparently, of the man, Stephen "naturally" turns to the one other man of her acquaintance. Step by step Stephen's determination grows into an obsession which has so compelling a hold on her imagination and pride that she thinks of nothing else. In this lengthy middle section of the novel Stoker is at his best, allowing time and detail fully to explore the minds and personalities of the three major characters. His rendering of Stephen's mingled pride, determination and diffidence is superb, enabling the reader to sympathize with her sense of mission and her strength of will while recognizing the error of her judgment if not of her theory. Little in Stoker's work

is as excrutiatingly painful as the proposal scene in which Stephen
is forced by Leonard's callous unconsciousness into greater explicitness than even she intended or as the following days in which
Stephen excoriates herself with self-loathing and shame which
assault her "wave upon wave." Unable to share her humiliation
and pain with anyone, hiding her anguish from her Aunt Laetitia,
and attempting to fulfill her daily obligations, Stephen cannot find
comfort even in the temporary solace of tears, the tears available
only to real women, as later becomes apparent.

Having brutally refused Stephen's proposal although he wants
her to pay his debts as she has offered, Leonard begins to recognize
his stupidity—his only saving grace in the reader's eyes for, had he
accepted Stephen, she would have married him despite subsequent
revelations regarding his character. Characteristically, his response
is to get drunk and to brag of his conquest of Stephen to none
other than Harold. At first incredulous, Harold is forced to believe
that Stephen has proposed when he sees her letter to Leonard
asking for a meeting and when he hears the ring of truth in
Leonard's voice. Devastated by his loss, Harold spends a sleepless
night trying to understand Stephen. Knowing her as he does, he
correctly concludes that she does not love Leonard; rather, he surmises, she has been testing a theory. Moreover, he understands her
humiliation and determines to offer himself up as a sacrifice to her
pride, deciding to propose so she can have the sense of superiority
gained by turning him down. This psychology, however, is somewhat facile, as Harold discovers, for his proposal meets with horror,
outrage, contempt, Stephen comprehending instantly that Harold
knows all. Tortured by her profound mortification, Stephen strikes
out at the one person who could provide the comfort she needs.
And Harold is forced by his generosity and naiveté to listen to the
woman he adores tell him she wishes she never met him and
would never see him again.

At this point the complication of the novel is wrought to its
greatest degree, marking also the beginning of the resolution. The
first element to be resolved is Leonard, who poses a threat to
Stephen by knowing of her shame, but who also sorely needs his

debts paid, debts of which his father cannot and will not relieve him. Stephen has agreed to pay these debts and, in a series of brilliant scenes narrated primarily from within Leonard's selfish perspective, Stephen gains the upper hand and evades his simultaneous blackmailing and lovemaking. A rather lengthy quotation from the text serves to indicate the mastery of motivation and narration Stoker achieves here, employing dialogue which distinguishes characters, tones both comic and ominous, and the narrative technique of *erlebte rede*, or free indirect speech, in which the narrator moves in and out of the character's thought patterns:

As he spoke, his words seemed, even to him, to be out of place. He felt that it would be necessary to throw more fervour into the proceedings. . . .

"Oh, Stephen, don't you know that I love you? You are so beautiful! I love you! I love you! Won't you be my wife?"

This was getting to much too close quarters. Stephen said in a calm, business like way:

"My dear Leonard, one thing at a time! I came out here you know, to speak of your debts; and until that is done, I really won't go into any other matter. Of course if you'd rather not. . . ." Leonard really could not afford this; matters were too pressing with him. . . .

"All right! Stephen. Whatever you wish I will do; you are the Queen of my heart, you know!"

"How much is the total amount?" said Stephen.

. . . He had come prepared to allow Stephen to fall into his arms, fortune and all. But now, although he had practical assurance that the weight of his debts would be taken from him, he was going away with his [tail] between his legs. He had not even been accepted as a suitor, he who had himself been wooed only a day before. His proposal of marriage had not been accepted, had not even been considered by the woman who had so lately broken iron-clad convention to propose marriage to him. . . . He had even been treated like a bad boy. . . . And all the time he dare not say anything lest the thing shouldn't come off at all. Stephen had such an infernally masterly way with her! . . . He would have to put up with it, till he had got rid of his debts! He never even considered the debt which he must still owe to

her. When that time came he would. . . . Well, he would deal with
some people and some things in a different way from that which he
had to do now! (*M*)

Stephen has shared some of her shameful secret with her aunt
Laetitia who, also knowing Leonard, deems it advisable to pay
Leonard's debts in her own name and with her own money. Together
the two women outwit and outmanoeuver the now pathetic Leonard.

The major element to be resolved is, of course, the relationship
between Stephen and Harold, but Harold takes Stephen at her word
and goes directly from his last meeting with her to London and
from there ships out to Alaska on a symbolically named cargo
vessel, the *Scoriac*. The balance of the story shifts here from Stephen
to Harold as Stoker narrates his version of the quest myth in
which the hero seeks his fortune in the typical forms, first, of a
treasure of gold and, then, of the princess. Before making his
fortune in the Alaskan goldfields, however, Harold wins the undying affection and gratitude of the Stonehouses, husband and wife
and their tiny daughter Pearl (doubtless influenced by Hawthorne's
Pearl), when during a tremendous storm Pearl is washed overboard
and Harold rescues her. Little Pearl is, of course, a delightful child
and reminds Harold of the girl Stephen was when he first met her.
Upon saving Pearl, Harold, traveling under the name John Robinson, is dubbed "the Man" by the child, and the reader has little
doubt that this rescue is prophetic. (In a rather bizarre scene,
Pearl spends the night in bed with Harold, since she only feels
safe when she's with him. Stoker is rather obsessively fastidious
about informing his readers when and where Harold puts on his
pyjamas and takes off his robe.) The next two years of Harold's
self-imposed exile are summarized rapidly as, refusing Mr. Stone-
house's offer to become a partner and, echoically, the son the Stonehouses never had, Harold makes his fortune founding Robinson
City in Alaska. At the end of that time, Harold boards a ship to
return to England via a northern route.

The two years have passed less eventfully for Stephen, though she
has had to face the implications of what she describes as her murder

of Harold. Shortly after ridding herself of Leonard, Stephen realized her behavior toward her best friend and advisor was far more shameful than that toward Leonard. "Sadly she turned over in her bed, and with shut eyes put her burning face on the pillow, to hide, as it were, from herself her abject depth of shame." Around the same time, Stephen is informed she has become the countess of Launoy (or Lannoy—the text has it both ways) and therefore owner of prodigious estates on the north coast of England. Aunt Laetitia, Stephen's beloved friend, dies at this time, after predicting that Stephen will find happiness at her new estate. Subsequently, Stephen decides to travel north and view her new land where her warmth and generosity make her beloved, where she takes long rides on her white mare, feeling happier—and more "feminine"—than she has in years, and where she meets and is befriended by the "Silver Lady," a Quaker who dresses all in silver grey. Becoming Stephen's counselor and comforter, the Silver Lady enables Stephen finally to find relief in tears.

Riding out one day as a storm threatens, Stephen sees a ship rushing perilously toward the rock-studded shore. Assisting in the rescue operations, she sees a large, athletic, bearded man save the ship by swimming toward port with the line tied to his waist. Although the ship is secured, the swimmer must return seaward or be dashed on the rocks. After considerable suspense and heroism on the part of many, Harold, for of course it is he, is brought ashore, alive but apparently blind. With the others rescued from the ship, he is brought to the Castle of the countess de Launoy where he recognizes Stephen's voice. She, however, does not recognize Harold under beard and bandages on the one occasion when she is allowed to see him, and Harold does not want her pity. Taking the doctor into his confidence. Harold forestalls for three weeks Stephen's desire to talk with him. At the end of this time, the Stonehouses arrive on the scene, Pearl having insisted that the great hero of the shipwreck was "the Man." The subsequent revelation scene includes Stephen fainting as she did once before when Harold saved her, as well as the discovery that Harold has regained his sight (shades of Jane Eyre and Rochester). But now that they are reunited,

one further barrier needs to be overcome. Recalling once more
the promise he made to Stephen's father, Harold wants Stephen
to make her own choice; but mindful of her earlier folly—and
now a real woman at long last able to weep tears—Stephen waits
for the man to speak first. Just as Aunt Laetitia helped Stephen
with Leonard, so now the Silver Lady helps with Harold, and the
two lovers are finally united.

Like *Miss Betty, The Man* is a novel with a message, a dominant
idea but, unlike the earlier novel, the idea in *The Man* is both more
problematic for Stoker and more interesting to his readers. While
both novels can be read as extended parables, based on a just
universe presided over by a benevolent divinity and informed
throughout by a judicious natural order, *The Man* complicates
plot through a detailed rendering of human emotion rather than
reducing it to a mechanical unwinding. Moreover, students of
Stoker's work as a whole will be fascinated by the direct examination of the nature and role of women which is a sustained though
more or less disguised concern of the other fiction. *The Man,* then,
provides explicit evidence of Stoker's ambivalence toward women.
Clearly fascinated by strong, intelligent, willful women—some of
the finest scenes are those in which Stephen bests Leonard—and
by the feminist concerns of his day, Stoker is determined to demonstrate the natural inferiority of Woman. Indeed, a contributing
factor to the contradictions in his portrayal of women is his effort
to force into the mold of Women the individual human being
whom his imagination recognizes as more distinctive than his
wishes or his message would like to allow. D. H. Lawrence was
to have similar difficulty very shortly thereafter and, in the novels
of both, tensions and contradictions between the dramatic and
the didactic components of the fiction are sources of strain and
weakness. Stoker seems conscious of difficulties in fitting the individual to the mold for, in the prologue to *The Man,* during a
proleptic debate between Stephen and Harold regarding woman's
ability to be just (here Stoker is making a case similar to that of
Freud in the 1905 *Essays on Sexuality*), Stoker comments: "But
sex is sex all through. It is not, like whiskers or a wedding ring,

a garnishment or maturity. Each little item of humanity gurgling in the cradle, or crowing when tossed in brawny arms, has a method of its own. For one sex there are thumpings, for the other, tears and such like blandishments. Not that either sex has an absolute monopoly of these means of accomplishing a wished-for end. But averages rule life" (*M*). In *The Man* Stoker attempts to demonstrate this axiom by portraying the evil attendant upon Stephen's behaving "like a man," specifically in proposing to Leonard. In a limited sense, Stoker provides a précis of the whole novel when he editorializes, "The punishment of her arrogant unwomanliness had, she felt, indeed begun" (*M*). It is precisely this sort of commentary which mars the novel's dramatic achievements. Elsewhere, Stoker describes Stephen's beauty as follows: "The hair, growing well down over the eyebrows, took away that look of barrenness which is often in a woman attendant on intellectually [*sic*] . . . (*M*). This view of the incompatibility of intelligence and sexual fertility in women is a standard Victorian conviction and is also demonstrated vividly in the character of Mina Harker in *Dracula* who has a "male mind" and no female sexuality.

Yet, the book is both richer and more complicated than this. Stoker takes pains to indicate the greatest problem lies with Stephen's mistaking Leonard and acting on theory rather than affection and respect. Indeed, and paradoxically given the moral of the story, Stephen's attraction to Leonard is based on her misapprehension of him as a real man, resulting from his unique opposition to her when they were children: Stephen "thought that this was a real boy who was masterful. Every fibre in her little feminine body realized the fact" (*M*). Stephen mistakes selfishness for manliness. Only later does she recognize Harold's self-sacrifice for her as true virility—a rather unexpected conclusion for a novelist who seems to wish to reinforce stereotypes. Moreover, although the painful distance between Harold and Stephen at the end of the novel is a result of her newly found womanliness, their final understanding is dependent upon the intervention of a surrogate mother, as was Stephen's earlier liberation

from Leonard's plotting. Finally, Stephen's attractiveness lies in
her strengths, her ability to initiate, to dominate, and to act, not
just in her knowledge of when to submit. Her money and social
position as well as her childhood encouragement to behave like
a man, to be her father's son, confer power upon her, a power
and a strength of will which help her save Harold from the sea
at the end of the novel. Stephen's "masculine" behavior in fact
both defines her and is the source of delight to the men. Little Pearl
resembles her in nothing so much as in a sort of imperious
dominance.

Thus, *The Man* is a fascinating novel for students of Stoker's
fiction, and indeed of Victorian fiction, revealing as it does
Stoker's concern with the role of women, their power, their sources
of attraction, and their nature. Moreover, Stoker has come some
distance since *Dracula* in which Mina Harker, the perfect Victorian
woman, reviles those of her sex who, in putting themselves
forward, might even someday dare to propose to men! By 1905
Stoker is not so unsympathetic as Mina. In a series of discussions
between Stephen and her aunt Laetitia, Stephen avers the equal
responsibility of men for pregnancies, even when they are un-
wanted. Moreover, she is horrified by the behavior of the women
she sees at Oxford, both the proper women and the immoral,
and she delivers a speech reminiscent of Hawthorne at the end
of *The Scarlet Letter:* "Some day women must learn their own
strength, as well as they have learned their own weakness. . . .
It is bad women who seem to know men best, and to be able to
influence them most. . . . Why should good women leave power
to such as they? Why should good women's lives be wrecked for
a convention? . . . The time will come when women will not be
afraid to speak to men, as they should speak, as free and equal"
(*M*).

While the moral of the book may seem to belie the import of
these questions, they seem nevertheless to be sincere on Stoker's
part as well as on Stephen's. Moreover, Stoker himself appears
to ridicule women's education and role in Victorian society by
using a conservative Aunt Laetitia as a negative role model, a

woman who lost the love of her life as a result of not being able to speak out. Treating her satirically as the representative of proper Victorian society, the narrator comments, "In Miss Rowly's young days Political Economy was not a subject which ladies were supposed to understand. . . . As to physiology, it was simply a word in use amongst scientific men, and associated in ordinary minds with lint and scalpels and that new creation of man's mind 'anesthetic'—whatever it may mean. . . . 'Sex' or 'sexual' were not words which could be used lightly. . . . Why, in certain select circles, it was not becoming to even mention the word 'leg,' anything below the belt was spoken of as 'foot,' or 'feet'" (*M*). Stoker strikes a final blow against this manifestation of Victorianism when Stephen complains of her ignorance and Aunt Laetitia responds indignantly, "Ignorant! Of course you were ignorant. . . . Isn't it what we have all been devoting ourselves to effect ever since you were born" (*M*).

Again, Stoker's major achievement in *The Man* is a richness of characterization which belies the facile moralizing, a depth apparent in the fact that, despite these repressive elements in her character, Laetitia Rowly is a shrewd and heroic woman whose protective and loving relationship with her niece is rendered in most moving terms. This complexity is rendered down to the least significant of relationships as well. In a discussion of one of Stephen's governesses, Miss Howard, the narrator comments that, while Stephen in her childish ignorance scorns the woman and therefore proposes to learn all she can the better to maintain her contempt of Miss Howard, she learns rather to respect and pity her.

*The Man* is strengthened also by Stoker's characteristically vivid rendering of natural scenes and of suspense. The scenes of rescue, both of Pearl and of Harold, though ripe for melodrama, are instead noteworthy for dramatic depictions of the natural forces, enlisting our hopes and sympathies for the characters as we await with our breath caught in our throats despite our awareness of the inevitable happy endings. It is worth pointing out with regard to the rescue scene, not only that it is a motif often found in

Stoker's novels and linked to his own attempted rescue from the Thames of a suicide, but that Stoker's transatlantic travels were frequently beseiged by terrific storms and that he almost lost his wife and son in a shipwreck. The autobiographical element in the novel is, indeed, strong, for the descriptions of Harold An Wolf, especially as the bearded giant, match those of Stoker. Like Stoker, too, Harold graduates from Trinity (Cambridge, though, not Dublin) with honors both in academics and athletics. Stoker's projection of himself into Harold may be most obvious in a rather bitter comment directed against the charming, debonair young man Leonard has grown into, the type of man who avoids the awkward stage of "men made in a large pattern." *The Man* enacts a sibling rivalry resolved by the triumph and rewarding of the heroic, self-sacrificing and virtuous brother who is the true man and who, consequently, wins the esteem and love of—ultimately—a womanly woman. Despite the simple plot, the heavy-handed and contradictory moralizing, and the occasional overtelling, *The Man* is a strongly rendered story. Its greatest strength being its characterizations, it is unique among Stoker's novels which typically depend on the mysterious or horrifying elements of their plots to exert their fascination. Stoker is capable of being an astute psychologist, especially perceptive regarding unconscious workings of the psyche: "The mind of an earnest man works quickly when once it has been set in motion. It is as though 'unconscious cerebration' were perpetually tilling the whole estate of one's mind ready for some possible harvest. Data hitherto almost unnoticed comes in on every side. Facts half remembered, half forgotten loom up large. Deductions leading to a definite end follow memories which had themselves seemed final" (*M*). While many of Stoker's most general speculations about the cosmos and human history and destiny are animistic and naive or just plain silly some are fascinating, as in the foreshadowing of the work of Claude Levi-Strauss: "Morals require heat of some kind. They are hardly indigenous to the animal, natural man; but rather to the civilized man. Man does not progress on raw food. The heat of cooking food may be the first propulsive force toward the Nirvana."[6]

Despite the roughnesses, then, and the contradictions, or perhaps partially because of the latter, *The Man* is a compelling and rewarding novel, most fascinating among Stoker's romances and explicit in its representation of his preoccupations, especially the nature of women and the blurring of identity.

## Chapter Three
# The Fairy Tales

Stoker's first extended literary production, a collection of eight tales for children published in 1882[1] and entitled *Under the Sunset,* provides an appropriate introduction to the novels of horror written in later years, foreshadowing their Gothic imagery and symbolism, their emphasis on orality, their concern about the boundary between life and death, as well as the prevalence of Oedipal configurations and rivalries among their characters and Stoker's ambivalence toward his female characters introduced already.

In his essay on the collection, Douglas Street claims that the tales in *Under the Sunset* are "true original fairy tales," employing stock motifs and devices including "periodically · excessive moralizing and the often violent punishment of the evil and sinful"[2] and a "heightened concept of the family with its loyal parent-child, sister-brother interrelationships";[3] that in them one sees the influence on Stoker of others who worked in this and related genres—such as Dickens and Lewis Carroll—as well as the influence of those Stoker knew and loved—Tennyson, Browning, Walt Whitman, Charlotte Stoker, and Henry Irving; and that the tales are essential to full comprehension of the later works, especially of *Dracula.* This latter observation will be the focus of the present discussion, with special emphasis on fantasy content and techniques of the Gothic.

In the first few stories, beginning with the title story, Stoker creates a universe parallel to the everyday, a land of dreams in which the child can view Eden, the fall into sin, and the redemption; it is, then, a somewhat secularized version of *Paradise Lost* and *Paradise Regained,* written for children. The Land Under the

Sunset is a tropical oasis of goodness, cultivation, and fertility in the midst of a threatening wilderness, the source of sin and punishment and, some say, Death: "Some say that the giants who still exist, live there, and that all poisonous plants there grow. They say that there is a wicked wind there that brings out the seeds of all evil things and scatters them over the earth. . . . Others say that Famine lives there in the marshes, and that he stalks out when men are wicked—so wicked that the spirits who guard the land are weeping so bitterly that they do not see him pass" (*S*, 4–5).

The conflict of the story begins, as one might expect, when "the hearts of men grew cold and hard with pride in their prosperity" (*S*, 5). As a result, the "children of King Death," especially the "dreadfullest one of all . . . , Skooro," (*S*, 7) invade the Land Under the Sunset through the only entrance, the Portal, guarded by two duplicate adult angels and a child-angel named Chiaro, for light. Chiaro is informed that the All-Father will allow the Children of Death to enter the portal because "The All-Father is wiser than even the angels can conceive. He overthrows the wicked with their own devices, and he traps the hunter in his own snare. The Children of Death when they enter . . . shall do much good in the land . . . For lo! the hearts of the people are corrupt. . . . Some pain or grief or sadness must be to them, that so they may see the error of their ways" (*S*, 8). The task for the child-angel, Chiaro, is to maintain a vigilant surveillance on Skooro, so that, as light, he may detect the "pure and true" and "steal into their hearts and by [his] own glorious light to make the gloom of the Children of Death unseen and unknown" (*S*, 9). Thus, functioning as an embodiment of faith, a Christ-figure, Chiaro protects the good from sin and death, while the Children of Death "left a lesson for good in the hearts of the dwellers in the land" (*S*, 10). Like Milton, then, Stoker is here concerned to "justify the ways of God to Man." "Under the Sunset" thus rather charmingly defines the moral perimeters and the allegorical terms of the conflict in a world where the rest of the tales' adventures transpire, providing a proleptic analysis of the history the volume as a whole enacts.

The second story, "The Rose Prince," describes a land still

predominantly good and pure, though Stoker takes the opportunity to reveal and caution humorously against folly by peopling the court of King Mago with some very silly lords and advisors, such as Tufto, the court sycophant; Sartoris, the court dandy and clothes-horse; Gabbleander, the Polonius of Mago's court; and so forth. Stoker observes: "Children who wish to become good and great men or good and noble women, should try to know well all the people whom they meet. Thus they will find that there is no one who has not much of good; and when they see some great folly, or some meanness, or some cowardice, or some fault or weakness in another person, they should examine themselves carefully" (*S*, 16).

The adventure which follows is a version both of the myth of the hero and of the David and Goliath story. Threatened by a Giant stalking toward the country, the people first send out their army which is destroyed except for one who lives to tell the tale. There seems no place for the king to turn for assistance until his son volunteers to face the giant alone. Reluctantly, the king and a young orphaned princess he has adopted, who has been the prince's constant companion through childhood and youth, watch Prince Zaphir depart, arrayed in glorious armor. However, only when he lays down his sophisticated weapons and armor, like Faulkner's Ike McCaslin, in a gesture of humble recognition of God's will, does he meet and, David-like, defeat the giant with a stone slung from his sling-shot. Thus, the Rose Prince, so named for the rose given him by Princess Bluebell as he set out, insures the safety of a virtuous people.

The next story in the volume, entitled "The Invisible Giant," the one written in reflection of Charlotte Stoker's story of the plague in Sligo, provides a different version of essentially the same moral tale. Here, in the Land Under the Sunset, many years after the deaths of King Mago, Princess Bluebell and Prince Zaphir, the land and the people have become corrupted and greedy, whether they are rich and carefree or impoverished and starving. Consequently, the people can no longer recognize giants—the dangers of sinfulness—and are therefore more vulnerable to the giants. The heroes of this tale are a Noah-like figure, named Knoal, and a young orphan girl, Zaya, who still mourns the loss of her beloved mother. Like all the heroes of these stories, Zaya enjoys a harmonious relationship with the trees and flowers, the birds and bees, especially the birds to whom she sings and who speak to her. (The fairy-tale motif of helpful animals recurs throughout these tales.) In fact, Zaya appears to others to be like a bird and, while the boys tease her, Stoker remarks tellingly, "Indeed it would be well for some naughty little boys and girls if they were as good and harmless as the little birds that work all day long for their helpless baby birds, building nests and bringing food, and sitting so patiently hatching their little speckled eggs" (*S*, 40).

One day when the birds seem to have deserted Zaya and she is gazing mournfully out her window, she sees the hideous specter of a huge giant: "In the sky beyond the city she saw a vast shadowy form with its arms raised. It was shrouded in a great misty robe that covered it, fading away into the air so that she could only see the face and the grim, spectral hands" (*S*, 41). Alas, only Zaya who is pure of heart can see the giant and only old Knoal who has lived a long and virtuous life, believes her. Cassandra-like, the two attempt together to convince the unbelieving people "of the terrible plague that was coming upon them" (*S*, 45). However, the unbelievers and those who scorn and threaten Knoal and Zaya are punished. Finally, too, many of Zaya's birds and even old Knoal fall victim to the plague, the blind giant as Stoker describes it, before the giant departs, leaving Zaya unharmed.

In the description of the devastation left by the giant in its wake, we can see the hand of Charlotte Stoker in her son's lines. In the words of a letter she wrote to her son around 1872:

One house would be attacked and the next spared. There was no telling who would go next, and when one said good-bye to a friend he said it as if for ever. In a very few days, the town became a place of the dead. No vehicles moved except the cholera carts or doctors' carriages. Many people fled, and many of these were overtaken by the plague and died by the way. . . . On some days the cholera was more fatal than on others, and on those days we could see a heavy sulphurous looking cloud hang low over the house, and we heard that birds were found dead on the shores of Lough Gill.[4]

In Bram's description, "Knoal and Zaya did all they could to help the poor people, but it was hard indeed to aid them, for the unseen giant was among them, wandering through the city to and fro, so that none could tell where next he would lay his ice-cold hand. Some people fled away out of the city; but it was little use, for go how they would and fly ever so fast they were still within the grasp of the unseen giant. Ever and anon he turned their warm hearts to ice with his breath and his touch, and they fell dead" (*S,* 49).

The rest of the stories in *Under the Sunset,* though less well integrated with each other than the three discussed so far, are more unusual, imaginative, and bizarre. Moreover, they more vividly foreshadow the direction Stoker's later works take as well as his literary strengths and preoccupations.

The fourth in the volume, entitled "The Shadow Builder," is both an eerie rendering of the parallel universe concept depicted in "Under the Sunset" and a parable affirming the strength of a mother's love. The conflict is engaged between two combatants, the Shadow Builder who is both death, insofar as he rules over the Procession of the Dead Past, comprised of the shadows of persons and events as they existed in life, and life insofar as he creates the shadows of all things living; and the Mother, who seeks to keep her son from the future, i.e., death, and who ultimately saves her son from passing through the Gate of Dread into death. Like Demeter in ancient myth, the Shadow Builder can cause life and activity where he wishes or barren solitude where his gaze never falls. The Mother, too, is conceived dualistically, insuring life, but threatening death as well.

"The Shadow Builder" is alternately eerie and visionary, on the one hand, and maudlin and melodramatic, on the other. Passages proleptic of the Gothic descriptions of later novels are especially noteworthy, such as the depiction of the "lonely abode" of the Shadow Builder:

Here are all pictures that are most fair and most sad to see—the passing gloom over a sunny cornfield when with the breeze comes the dark sway of the full ears as they bend and rise; the ripple on the glassy surface of a summer sea; the dark expanse that lies beyond and without the broad track of moonlight on the water; the lace work of glare and gloom that flickers over the road as one passes in autumn when the moonlight is falling through the naked branches of overhanging trees; the cool, restful shade under the thick trees in summertime when the sun is flaming down on the haymaker at work; the dark clouds that flit across the moon, hiding her light, which leaps out again hollowly and coldly; the gloom of violet and black that rises on the horizon when rain is near in summertime; the dark recesses and gloomy caverns where the waterfall hurls itself shrieking into the pool below. . . . (*S*, 55).

The weakest section of the story is the portrayal of the undying love of the mother who moves mountains to rescue her shipwrecked son and who finally succeeds.[5] The story ends with the sentimental: "The lonely Shadow Builder knows now that the Mother's arms are stronger than the grasp of Death" (*S*, 71). But in its course it contains passages expressive of recurrent Stoker concerns. In it, in fact, we can locate Stoker's obsession with the boundary between life and death and the motif of rescue from death. These themes are tied here both to the strength and love of the mother and to an Oedipal configuration, for the Shadow Builder is the patriarchal creator who wishes to separate the boy from his mother. Ambiguously, while the rescue of the son at the end of the story seems a triumph, it can also be seen as regressive, though reluctantly so by Stoker. For just as the child is earlier seen to outgrow his mother's assistance in learning to walk, and again later, as the young man must break from his mother's grasp to depart for his future life, so death lies both in the mother's embrace and in the future.

The figure of the mother is central, powerful, even awesome in her dedication, at the same time as she is idealized, sentimentalized, and fictionalized: she is the perfect mother, insofar as she has no concerns other than those of her single son and she is able to protect him. Nevertheless, though less obviously, she is grasping and punitive, for she can create guilt in the child who is longing to leave her embrace for future adventures.

It might be argued, then, that "The Shadow Builder" reenacts a drama of ambivalence Stoker himself may have undergone when, as a sickly infant and child, he remained in bed through his seventh year. Certainly, it is the case that the later fictions reveal a preoccupation with death in life and life in death; in fact, as we shall see in our discussion of *The Lady of the Shroud*, Stoker is most explicit about the appearance of the living as if they were dead and the appearance of the dead as if alive, in that case, the hero's fiancée and mother, respectively (and in the case of *Dracula,* the vampires). The hero of *The Lady of the Shroud* asserts that one of the most universal desires, manifested in myth throughout time and culture, is the wish to bring back the dead. "The Shadow Builder" both fulfills and denies this fantasy as it portrays the pains and sorrows of growing up and old.

"The Shadow Builder" exists, like the other characters and adventures in the volume, in the land of dreams but, more than is the case with the former stories, in this one Stoker has correlated dreams with unconscious fantasies. For example, in describing the activities of the lonely Shadow Builder, Stoker says, "Sometimes from a sleeping body the Shadow Builder summons a dreaming soul; then for a time the quick and the dead stand face to face, and men call it a dream of the Past. When this happens, friend meets friend or foe meets foe; and over the soul of the dreamer comes a very happy memory long vanished, or the troubled agony of remorse" (*S*, 56). Thus, while the allegorical nature of the earlier stories persists, the rendering here is complicated and enriched by a psychological dimension.

In his later works, Stoker repeatedly refers to unconscious workings of the mind, a fact not so surprising in view both of the times and of the mode in which he writes. In a recent study of the Gothic genre, Elizabeth MacAndrew claims quite correctly that a distinguishing feature of nineteenth-century Gothic is the way in which the terrifying and uncanny external events and characters reveal the depths of the central characters' unconscious mental lives.[6] Certainly, this is true in Stoker's best works—indeed, the attribute is an indication of the richness of the work—though Stoker was not necessarily aware of the ways in which this was manifest, as we shall see especially with regard to his portrayal of the women in his fictional work.

As the hero of *The Lady of the Shroud* mentions in the passage referred to above, one of the most well-known versions of the myth of rescue from the dead is that of Orpheus and Eurydice, and in "The Castle of the King," the penultimate story in *Under the Sunset,* Stoker has written his own version of that story, one which in tone, imagery, and theme belongs with "The Shadow Builder." "The Castle of the King"[7] tells of a poet who strove all his youth to succeed in order to win the love of a rich maiden. After years of trial, the two are married and happy together but, while visiting an aged relative, the wife sickens and dies. When he is told his wife is now in the Castle of the King, the Poet sets off for the land beyond the Portal. Traveling through increasingly threatening landscapes populated by equally threatening animals, all vividly and imaginatively described, the Poet thinks only of his wife and of lessons he is learning for mankind.

Traveling on, the Poet reaches territory where even the snakes fear to follow: "The gloomy defiles whence issue the poisonous winds that sweep with desolation even the dens of the beasts of prey—the sterile fastnesses which march upon the valleys of desolation. Here even the stealthy serpents paused in their course. . . . They glided back, smiling with deadliest rancour, to their obscene clefts." The Poet travels still onward, to where "even solid things lost their substance, and melted in the dark and cold mists which swept along" (*S,* 108). As the Poet continues his travel and travail, he alternately despairs and hopes, but is carried forward even as he wearies. Finally, as he becomes too weak to continue much farther, and sinks in exhaustion to the ground, he sees the Castle rise up out of the mist before him and has a vision of his wife patiently awaiting him.

"The Castle of the King" is one of Stoker's most powerful stories, in fact, for in addition to the unified and sophisticated design of the story, over and above Stoker's typically powerful rendering of nightmarish visions, there is an incantatory, almost hypnotic quality to the rhythm with which the prolonged journey of the Poet is evoked. Only at the very end does the reader recognize with a start that the journey is an imaginary one, even an allegorical one, tracing the death of the Poet (mythically portrayed as a journey throughout literature and dream). The Castle appears, like Count Dracula, first as a mist—"Forth from the marsh before him crept a still, spreading mist. It rose silently, higher—higher—enveloping the wilderness for far around" (*S,* 115)—then, as "a ray of light shot upward . . . as it struck the summit of the Castle keep the Poet's spirit in an instant of time swept along the causeway. Through the ghostly portal of the Castle it swept, and met with joy the kindred spirit that it loved. . . ." Just as swiftly the story concludes, dissolving in a "lightning's flash" Castle and vision and disclosing "a fair garden where, among the long summer grass lay the Poet, colder than the marble statues around him" (*S,* 116–17). Stoker's control is remarkable here as he correlates the dream vision with the psychological state, one hallmark of the Gothic.

In considering a correlation among these early stories, the later novels, and Stoker's unconscious fantasy life, it would be difficult to exceed the imaginative effort of Joseph S. Bierman who, in a study entitled *"Dracula:* Prolonged Childhood Illness, and the Oral Triad,"[8] argues for positive correlations among *Dracula,* two stories from *Under the Sunset,* and Stoker's childhood malaise and his position in his family.

The story in *Under the Sunset* following "The Shadow Builder" and the first Bierman discusses is "How 7 Went Mad," a tale about a young boy named Tineboy who hates to do his multiplication tables, especially when the number 7 is involved, and his pet raven, Mr. Daw, a name Stoker uses again, significantly enough in his *The Jewel of Seven Stars,* where a Sergeant Daw investigates a mystery filled with sevens. Here, Tineboy lies his head on his desk at school, ostensibly to think better, while Mr. Daw looks on from a tree, and he falls asleep. Tineboy dreams that his teacher is telling a story explaining how number 7 went mad as a consequence of mistreatment and loneliness: 7 says, "I am wrong added, wrong divided, wrong subtracted, and wrong multiplied. Other numbers are not treated as I am; and, besides, they are not orphans like me. . . . Number 2 . . . never gets into any trouble and 4, 6, and 8 are his cousins. Number 3 is close to 6 and 9. Number 5 is half a decimal and he never gets in trouble. But as for me, I am miserable, ill-treated, and alone" (*S*, 80–81). Through his sobs, 7 explains his situation to the Alphabet Doctor and to all the other numbers in the Numbers Stables in a scene reminiscent of Lewis Carroll. The numbers are housed in stables because "they go so fast": Look at your multiplication table; it starts with twice one are two, and before you get down the page you are at twelve times twelve" (*S*, 76). The Doctor examines 7 with a stethoscope, a telescope, a microscope, and a horoscope, using each in a manner opposite to its intended use. As the Doctor explains, " 'When one is insane, the fact of the disease necessitates an opposite method of treatment.' Then he took the telescope and looked at him to see how near he was, and the microscope to look how small; and then he drew his horoscope" (*S*, 78). In this looking-glass world of Tineboy's dream, the bad boy, Tineboy's double named Ruffin, still claims he wishes 7 had died, despite the new sympathy for 7 evoked in the other children, including Tineboy. After school, Mr. Daw, who has entered the classroom while no one was looking, remains behind and eats up all the 7's he can find. When the children return the next day, an hour late, they perceive something is missing, but they can't tell what until Mr. Daw begins to vomit up 7's which are compulsively multiplied (in one case incorrectly so, though Street's edition corrects the error). At the end of the story, Tineboy awakens with the correct answer to the problem which had originally put him to sleep and with an affection for the forlorn, orphaned 7.[9]

The second story from *Under the Sunset* which Bierman refers to, and the last one in the volume, is one in which the Oedipal components and rivalries are far more obvious. "The Wondrous Child" tells of two young children, a boy and girl, of the lord of the manor of a peaceful village. The boy, Sibold, is just eight years old and his sister, May, is almost six (thus, again, the number 7 is missing). They are great comrades, these two, sharing games, dreams, and secret haunts, their favorite a bower "under a great weeping willow. This was a mighty tree, many hundreds of years old, which towered aloft above the other trees which dotted the sward. The long branches fell downwards so thickly, that even in winter, when the leaves had fallen and the branches were bare, one could hardly see into the hollow that lay within" (S, 119). This hidden and womblike hollow, difficult of access, is full of gorgeous flowers including "Tulips, opening their mouths to the sun and the rain; for the tulip is a greedy flower, that opens his mouth till at last he opens it so wide that his head falls all to pieces and he dies" (S, 121; an interesting image indeed!).

After this exposition, the story proper opens on one particular day which is a holiday for the children because "A tiny boy brother had arrived in the house, and everybody was busy getting things for him" (S, 121). Sibold and May's response to the new arrival is to "look and look till they found a baby too . . . , [to] search for another little baby all for themselves" (S, 122). Planning to have lunch in their favorite haunt, May and Sibold gather flowers and leaves to make a throne and crown for their baby brother to proclaim him "king of the feast." After decorating their bower with poppies, leaves, and a tiger lily, May and Sibold fall asleep and dream of sailing away past beautiful flowered lands to an especially lovely spot where May wishes to look for parsley, "Because if there was a nice bed of parsley we might be able to find a baby— And oh, Sibold, I *do* so want a baby."[10] Of course, May and Sibold find a baby almost immediately, but just as quickly, they begin to argue over whose baby it is: "Look here, you know, I found that baby; he belongs to me.' [Sibold is several times presented as a bit of a pompous ass.] 'Oh please,' said May, 'I heard him first. He is mine.' 'He is mine,' said Sibold; 'He is mine,' said May; and both began to get a little angry" (S, 129). This argument, they find to their horror, has killed the baby; but, being a miraculous infant, he revives when May and Sibold apologize to each other.

The new family constellation formed by this threesome is quite explicit, with the baby calling May "little mother" and with Sibold attempting to provide food and shelter for the other two. Indeed, protection is especially necessary, for the three are threatened by, first, a ferocious tiger (recall the tiger-lily), then, an "enormous serpent, with small eyes that shone like sparks of fire, and two great open jaws. These jaws were so big that it really seemed as if the beast's whole head opened in two [recall the tulip]; and between them appeared a great forked tongue which seemed to spit venom" (*S*, 135). The serpent is followed noisily by a "mighty bird of prey" and a shark and a crocodile, the shark with "its triple rows of great teeth grinding together" and the crocodile with "its terrible mouth . . . opening and shutting, snapping its big teeth together." Finally, a nearby volcano erupts and out of its lava-riven crater emerges "the head of a fiery dragon, with eyes like burning coals [a description familiar from *Dracula*] and teeth like tongues of flame" (*S*, 137). But at the sight of "the wondrous child" all anger is quelled, all threat disappears, and these animals, and others now joining in droves, devote themselves to protecting the child. At this, May and Sibold decide the child must be an angel, and grow fearful at the liberties they have taken. Apologizing to the baby, May observes with regard to the animals surrounding them, "do not they all look nice and pretty sitting around like that? . . . I wish they would always be like that, and never fight nor disagree at all, dear Ba" (*S*, 139). "Ba" responds to May's whispered apology for having addressed him so familiarly, "Be always loving and sweet, dear child, and even the angels will know your thoughts and listen to your words" (*S*, 140). Filled with happiness, May and Sibold sail back to their bower where, "both feeling sleepy, they put their arms around each other, and lay down to rest" (*S*, 142).

The only explicit point Bierman makes about this story is that of the child found on a bed of parsley which he feels correlates with the "oral triad" of eating, sleeping, and being eaten (as well as with the report that Stoker had the dream which inspired *Dracula* after eating dressed crab which, Bierman observes, was often served on a bed of parsley). Clearly, however, many of the other motifs found elsewhere in Stoker, some of which Bierman discusses, are present also in this story. The tale begins with the rivalry of May and Sibold with the new baby brother, the arrival of whom leaves them, neglected, to their own devices. The rivalry first takes the form of a competitive desire for their own baby and then antagonism toward each other resulting from possessiveness about the infant they discover. Their hostility is then projected outward onto the devouring animals which threaten the original object of rivalry, the infant, as well as May and Sibold themselves, but the events act out a sublimation of the hostility, transforming it into protectiveness, in the face of perhaps magical powers of the infant. This sublimation provides a satisfactory resolution of the initial conflict, as harmony is established in both the animal kingdom and the human. Thus, as Bierman implies, the motif of aggression against a rival, sibling or filial, is evident in this story and, indeed, manifested in oral terms, with particular emphasis on the appearance and sound of (here animal and floral) mouths, teeth, and eyes. The underlying fantasies and anxieties include both the desire to eat and to be devoured placed within the contexts both of dream-sleep and of sibling rivalry and hostility toward parents. Whether Bierman is correct in his speculations regarding the specific autobiographical sources of these fantasies, certainly the desires, anxieties, displacements, and sublimations recur throughout Stoker's fictions, most dramatically in *Dracula.*

In addition, then, to demonstrating the ways in which Stoker works within the fairy tale genre, the stories in *Under the Sunset,* all but one of which have been discussed here,[11] are of assistance in corroborating an analysis of the most striking characteristics of Stoker's later and longer fiction: the preoccupation with Oedipal rivalries and configurations, the ambivalence toward women, the employment of Gothic imagery and symbolism, the recurrence of oral imagery, and the concern about the boundary between life and death. While the tales can indeed be read for both entertainment and instruction by young readers, it is the more complex and unusual among them which are of interest to those examining Stoker's work as a whole.

## Chapter Four
# The Horror Tales

Stoker's tales of horror and mystery—*The Jewel of Seven Stars* (1903), *The Lady of the Shroud* (1909), and *The Lair of the White Worm* (1911)—all written after *Dracula,* are romances as well, and to the extent that each is a romance, it resembles those stories dealt with in the chapter on romances, employing the same idealizations of heroes and heroines, the same ambivalences regarding women, the same Oedipal configurations, and most often the same sentimental resolutions in which the hero and heroine are united in a clasp which embraces a father or father figure as well. Heroines are typically extraordinarily beautiful, virtuous, intelligent and obedient; the heroes are almost all, like Stoker, large, strong, and brave beyond the norm. As we have seen, the romance plot, so conceived, wears thin rapidly and the strengths of Stoker's fiction derive rather from descriptions of natural and preternatural scenes and from the development and sustaining of suspense. In the tales of horror, the convenient and often heavy-handed motif of mistaken or confused identity recurrent throughout the romances assumes an uncanny force as it becomes the merging or blurring of identities, one of the most significant elements in Stoker's creation of the fantastic and, we will suggest later, in his life as well. Additionally, the blurring of identities is linked, in the horror tales, to a concern about the boundary between life and death.[1]

Not surprisingly, then, those tales of mystery and horror in which the elements of the preternatural and uncanny outweigh the romantic are the more compelling and more successful. This is easy to demonstrate in relation to these novels and doing so will enhance our understanding of what makes *Dracula* Stoker's supreme fiction and the continued success it is.

### The Jewel of Seven Stars

None of the novels written subsequently is as good as *Dracula,* though several are fascinating in their own ways, especially *The Jewel of Seven Stars,* written during 1902.[2] Moreover, Stoker's talents as a researcher and his skill in employing the fruits of his research serve him well in creating the uncanniness of his tale. In *Jewel* Stoker has taken great pains not only to describe Egyptian objects and metaphysics in full detail and with considerable accuracy, but also to provide such a wealth of detail about the mysterious Queen Tera, her plans, and her tomb that reader credulity is readily enlisted, especially that of the reader who recognizes the names of Wallis Budge and other Egyptologists, the names of Hathor, Ptah-Seker-Ausar, and other Egyptian deities, as well as the analysis of the "several parts of a human being . . . the Ka or Double, the Ba (the soul of Ka), the Khu (spirit), the Sekhem (power), the Kaibit (shadow), the Ren (name), the Khat (physical body), and the Ab (heart)" quoted from Budge.[3] Clearly, Stoker has done his research, and *Jewel* is a novel with which he took some pains.

In *Jewel,* Stoker duplicates the romance of the endangered woman rescued by a small group of men, both older and younger, which he first employed in *Dracula.* As in *Dracula,* the plot of *Jewel* is complicated by the doubling of the female protagonist and by ambivalence toward her. The ending in particular expresses this ambivalence clearly and is less satisfactory, though as interesting as the ending of *Dracula.* The narrative technique of *Jewel* is far simpler than the journal-letter format Stoker employs in *Dracula* and elsewhere, though the innocent-I account of Malcolm Ross is highly effective in building and sustaining suspense.

The novel opens as Malcolm is summoned from his sleep by a persistent and ominous knocking at his door. Called to the home of a beautiful woman he has met only twice before, Margaret Trelawny, Ross discovers that she hopes for his help in discovering the cause of a mysterious attack on her father which has left him with a bizarre wound on the same wrist on which he wears a key soldered to a bracelet. Discovered in a pool of blood beside an iron safe in his bedroom, Trelawny is in a cataleptic trance from which he cannot be roused for four days. During those four days, the mystery deepens as the attacks on Mr. Trelawny are repeated, as the doctor observes that the slashes on Trelawny's wrist are made by a seven-clawed creature, as Scotland Yard is called in, and as Malcolm observes his own increasing fascination both with the ancient Egyptian objects in Trelawny's house and with Margaret herself. By the time Mr. Trelawny awakens, the mysteries are absolutely obscure. Malcolm and Margaret have tacitly understood their mutual affection. Both the detective and the doctor have separately voiced to Malcolm suspicions of Margaret's complicity in the attacks on her father, and Malcolm is torn between his love for her and the force of the evidence (he is a lawyer): Margaret is the first one to find her father after the attacks, she appears at inconvenient moments, and she has a pet to whom she is devoted, a seven-toed cat, which makes a frenzied assault on an ancient cat mummy every time it is allowed into Mr. Trelawny's bedroom. Moreover, a Mr. Corbeck, an associate of Mr. Trelawny, comes on the scene announcing that he has located, after many years of effort, seven lamps in search of which Mr. Trelawny had sent him. These lamps have mysteriously disappeared from Corbeck's hotel room, but they reappear, equally mysteriously, in Margaret's sitting room.

The complexity of the mystery, and its uncanniness, is heightened by the nature of Mr. Trelawny's and Corbeck's studies and experiences as well as by the nature of the objects in Trelawny's bedroom. The lamps are the final equipment Trelawny has needed to fulfill his great experiment, one which the reader learns of as Margaret, Malcolm, and Dr. Winchester do. The rest of the necessary objects have already been collected and placed in the bedroom, including the jewel of seven stars—an enormous ruby carved like a scarab and containing seven stars in the exact contemporary position of the stars in the constellation of the Plough—a great stone sarcophagus and "Magic Coffer," sharing similar hieroglyphics, carved gaps, and protuberances, and most ghastly, both the mummy of a great Egyptian queen and the severed hand of the mummy, a beautiful, dusky white, perfectly preserved hand—with seven digits! The mummy and hand are those of "Tera, Queen of the Egypts, daughter of Antef. Monarch of the North and South, Daughter of the Sun. Queen of the Diadems" (*J*, 161), a remarkable "historical" figure who was adept, not only in statecraft, but in ancient magic and ritual and all the Egyptian sciences. Locked in a battle with the priests of her day and representing the powers existing before the gods, Tera determined to suspend herself in time, making all preparations necessary for her resurrection centuries later. The time has come for her project to be fulfilled, and this is the great experiment in which Mr. Trelawny is engaged.

The mystery does not end here, however, for while Trelawny's discovery of Tera's tomb hidden in the "Valley of the Sorcerers" was not the first, it was intimately bound up with his own life. Leaving his young and pregnant wife at home, Trelawny had set off for the tomb and, while he was in the burial chamber itself, his wife died in childbirth, their daughter being delivered from her dead body. Margaret does not, we are told, resemble her mother; rather, she looks strikingly like the portraits of Queen Tera; moreover, for birthmark she has a jagged scar across one wrist, though she has only the normal number of fingers. Gradually, Malcolm must come to terms with the realization that Margaret's body is inhabited both by her own spirit and by that of Queen Tera as well and, as the time determined for the great experiment approaches, she is less and less his and more and more the queen's.

Central to the conception and the mystery of the novel is a complex of familiar motifs: the ambivalence toward the female and the mergings or doublings of identity. Here, too, *Jewel* manages these elements adeptly. Margaret's involvement with the attacks on her father is skillfully done: we must suspect her a little but suspicion must not lead too quickly to a recognition of her identity with Queen Tera, nor must either Tera or Margaret be viewed as essentially dangerous and threatening until the right moment. Stoker handles this problem both by the involved narrator and by establishing Margaret's ignorance of her father's life and studies:

she has only recently come to live with him. Thus, Stoker is able to maintain Margaret's essential innocence at the same time that he prepares for her doubling with the powerful, numinous Queen Tera, and for the resolution which, in effect, purifies the woman.

Perhaps even more subtly, Stoker employs the archetype of the journey into the realm of the fantastic, the realm of dreams, nightmares, and encounters with doubles, by use of foil characters and magical spaces. As the novel opens, the narrator is in his own home and asleep, recapitulating in his dreams his brief meetings with Margaret Trelawny. The first paragraph itself establishes the dream-memory as a shadowing forth of the resurrection motif: "It all seemed so real that I could hardly imagine that it had ever occurred before; and yet each episode came, not as a fresh step in the logic of things, but as something expected. It is in such wise that memory plays its pranks for good or ill . . . It is thus that life is bittersweet, and that which has been done becomes eternal" (*J, 9*). Malcolm continues significantly: "For it is in the arcana of dreams that existences merge and renew themselves, change and yet keep the same—like the soul of a musician in a fugue. And so memory swooned, again and again, in sleep" (*J*, 10). The threshold crossing into the world of dreams is repeated in the threshold crossing into the Trelawny household where Malcolm, as it were, rejoins his dreams in a magical space. The sacredness of the space is reinforced and reaffirmed through a series of events, including the expelling of the uninitiated and the inward movement toward an even more sanctified arena: the labyrinthine path the mystery figuratively traces is literally acted out in the characters' movement through space in the novel.

Two significant though minor characters function further to demarcate the magical space of the dream world in *Jewel*. Most obvious is the world-renowned medical authority called in for a consultation about Trelawny by Margaret. This older male authority recalls *Dracula*'s Van Helsing but, unlike the latter, Sir James Frere, as he is significantly named,[4] voices the skeptical views of modern science, and is willing to take the case only on the condition that the magical space be violated. Either Trelawny or the Egyptian artifacts must be moved from his room. This, of course, is precisely the tabooed act, prohibited by Trelawny in a letter written prior to the first attack on him. Frere is denied his condition and ejected from the magical space. However, the attending physician, a Dr. Winchester, agrees not only to stay but to see it to the end, thus maintaining the circle of initiates.

Similarly, the character of Nurse Kennedy, originally brought in to attend Trelawny, is also removed from the inner circle. During her first night watching by the bedside, Nurse Kennedy is sent into a trance resembling Trelawny's. This bit of business seems, on the whole, gratuitous, except for the fact that Nurse Kennedy, too, embodies rationality and common sense. Moreover, she is introduced in a crucial passage in which she is described in vivid detail as a foil to Margaret and Margaret's type of beauty. The significance of the contrast is heightened both by the detail in which it is described by the narrator and by its location at the very beginning of the third chapter:

By comparison of the two I seemed somehow to gain a new knowledge of Miss Trelawny. Certainly, the two women made a good contrast. Miss Trelawny was of fine figure; dark, straight-featured. She had marvellous eyes; great, wide-open, and as black and soft as velvet, with a mysterious depth. To look in them was like gazing at a black mirror such as Doctor Dee used in his wizard rites. . . . The eyebrows were typical. Finely arched and rich in long curling hair, they seemed like the proper architectural environment of the deep, splendid eyes. Her hair was black also, but was as fine as silk. Generally black hair is a type of animal strength and seems as if some strong expression of the forces of a strong nature; but in this case there could be no such thought. There were refinement and high breeding; and though there was no suggestion of weakness, any sense of power there was, was rather spiritual than animal. The whole harmony of her being seemed complete. Carriage, figure, hair, eyes; the mobile full mouth, whose scarlet lips and white teeth seemed to light up the lower part of the face—as the eyes did the upper; the wide sweep of the jaw from chin to ear; the long, fine fingers; the hand which seemed to move from the wrist as though it had a sentience of its own. All these perfections went to make up a personality that dominated either by its grace, its sweet-ness, its beauty, or its charm.

Nurse Kennedy, on the other hand, was rather under than over a woman's average height. She was firm and thickset, with full limbs and broad, strong, capable hands. Her colour was in the general effect that of an autumn leaf. The yellow-brown hair was thick and long, and the golden-brown eyes sparkled from the freckled, sunburnt skin. Her rosy cheeks gave a general idea of rich brown. The red lips and white teeth did not alter the colour scheme, but only emphasised it. She had a snub nose—there was no possible doubt about it; but like such noses in general it showed a nature generous, untiring, and full of good-nature. Her broad white forehead, which even the freckles had spared, was full of forceful thought and reason. (*J,* 31–32)

Nurse Kennedy is nothing if not the antithesis of mystery and uncanniness, the rejection of purely "animal" spirits and power, and she, too, is removed from the magical space.

During the rest of the novel others are ejected, singly and in groups: namely, Sergeant Daw[5] from Scotland Yard and most of the servants. Finally, the circle of the initiated moves to Trelawny's secret castle, through winding passages into an enormous cave by the sea to perform the great experiment. This circle includes, of course, Margaret, Trelawny and Malcolm Ross, and Dr. Winchester and Mr. Corbeck as well. Thus, we have a configuration similar to that of *Dracula,* though without the marked Oedipal and sibling rivalry of the earlier novel, in which a band of men, led by a father figure (here actually the father), dedicate themselves to saving the woman.

Mr. Trelawny's preparations for the experiment are fascinating and elaborate. Equally compelling is the suspense Stoker builds as the time for the consummation of Tera's and Trelawny's dream approaches. The first-person narration is exceptionally effective, for Malcolm more than anyone else is attuned to the changes in Margaret and therefore to the presence of the spirit of Queen Tera. The personality alterations Margaret undergoes are, to him, un-canny and terribly distressing as he recognizes the possibility that, should Tera arise, she might not be submissively grateful for the assistance she has received. Indeed, the chances are that she will not be, for, in unguarded moments, as her spirit dominates Margaret's, Malcolm has seen Margaret fall "into a positive fury of passion. Her eyes blazed, and her mouth took on a hard, cruel tension which was new to me" (*J,* 208). And this, in response to her own cat's attack on Tera's familiar, the cat mummy.

How then, is this doubling, and the novel, to be resolved? As in the case of *Dracula,* the solution is the destruction of the violent woman. The alternations Margaret manifests closely resemble those of Lucy Westenra; the spirit of the vampire, with all its seductive force, is that of Queen Tera, the other side of the submissive, loving wife. Moreover, the similarity extends to the questioning of the animation of the entombed body and to the sexuality of the "dead" woman: in *Jewel,* Margaret recognizes this sexuality when she objects to the striptease Tera is forced to provide as her body is robbed of its wrappings. As in *Dracula,* the undead and sexually threatening woman is destroyed. While Trelawny's surmises are accurate and the spirit of Tera returns to her flesh as she begins to rise, mysteriously the resurrection is aborted: all that remains of Tera is a handful of dust.[6]

The rather lame ending seems weak in part because of the success of the rest of the novel. From the very first the mysteriousness, the uncanniness is unremitting; all details are revealed in their place, not before, all seem essential, and all build toward the one climax. The reader is led to credit it all by the sheer force of the detail Stoker provides, based both on his own research and on stories of Egypt and Egyptology heard at the table of Sir William Wilde, Oscar Wilde's father.[7]

Enhanced by identification with the narrator who learns as we learn and who has human doubts and anxieties, reader assent in the fantasy is optimal. Moreover, our desire for the consummation of the great experiment is strong: only that will resolve the novel. But, through Malcolm's distress, we are also concerned about the potential destructiveness of the terrible Tera, so we alternately wish for failure, or at least, escape.

Not surprisingly, however, the final paragraphs, reasserting the romance component of the story, are anticlimactic. Moreover, they hark back to the weakest section of the novel, the section in which, as if in a trance, Margaret pours forth her convictions about Tera's motivation for arranging her resurrection:

"I can see her in her loneliness and in the silence of her mighty pride, dreaming her own dream of things far different from those around her. . . . A land of wholesome greenery, far, far away. Where were no scheming and malignant priesthood; whose ideas were to lead to power through gloomy temples and more gloomy caverns of the dead, through an endless ritual of death! A land where love was not base, but a divine possession of the soul! Where there might be some one kindred spirit which could speak to hers through mortal lips like her own; whose being could merge with hers in a sweet communion of soul to soul, even as their breaths could mingle in the ambient air! . . ." (*J*, 190)

Margaret is clearly projecting, here, saying that she knows what Tera dreamed of now that such a love has come into her own life; moreover, the imagery suggests that Tera's motivation is to move from the heated passion and violence of the desert to the purified, spiritualized, Edenic innocence of a Northern love, such a migration reflecting the novel's transformation of Margaret as well. Transcending the personal level of romance, the care and effort taken both by Tera and by Trelawny in executing the great experiment seem to warrant a more universally significant motivation, just as the genius and power of the woman requires greater scope than that afforded by the quest for a Prince Charming. Indeed, toward the climax of the novel, Mr. Trelawny remarks, "What is a woman's life in the scale with what we hope for! . . . Imagine what it will be for the world of thought—the true world of human progress— . . . if there can come back to us out of the unknown past one who can yield to us the lore stored in the great Library of Alexandria . . . we can be placed on the road to the knowledge of lost arts, lost learning, lost sciences . . ." (*J*, 219–20).

We see again, then, that Stoker's power lies with the mysterious and uncanny and that his novels succeed to the degree that the romance components are subordinated to those of the fantastic. Further, we recognize the basic plot pattern employed in *Jewel* and in Stoker's other tales of terror: ostensibly directed toward saving the female, in this case almost giving birth to her, the journey in *Jewel* has as its underlying function the need to come to terms with ambiguous female nature. As in *Dracula,* the confrontation entails the destruction of the dangerous dimension of the woman. As Tera dies, so too does her spirit in Margaret, and the novel ends with Margaret's and Malcolm's marriage and with a return to the daylight. Margaret's last words bring us out of the dream, out of the magical space in which we confront the double and our fears and desires about the female which the novel has portrayed: "Do not grieve for her! Who knows, but she may have found the joy she sought? Love and patience are all that make for happiness in this world; or in the world of the past or of the future; of the living or the dead. She dreamed her dream; that is all that any of us can ask!" (*J*, 254).

The relationship between *Dracula* and *The Jewel of Seven Stars* is that of sharply etched original to paler copy. *Jewel* transforms the obvious violence and sexuality—both as they are desired and abhorred—of the pre-Oedipal battle of its precursor into a milder, more highly intellectualized and consequently less dramatic rendering. *Jewel* is, then, both a strong novel on its own, and a fascinating and enlightening counterpart to *Dracula.*

### The Lady of the Shroud

In 1909 Stoker published *The Lady of the Shroud,*[8] a novel set, at its outset, in January of the preceding year. Like the other tales of horror, *The Lady of the Shroud* begins in the domain of the fantastic and gradually dissipates the uncertainty felt by the protagonist and the reader, this time in the direction of the naturalistic: there is, in other words, a rational explanation for the mystery. Employing a resolution somewhat like that of *Jewel* insofar as its mystery is finally explicable in terms of purported human possibility, though *Jewel* requires us to believe in a science in advance of our own and a couple of supernatural elements, *The Lady of the Shroud* does not sustain the mystery and mood of eeriness to its conclusion. Moreover, although it employs a variety of narrative devices similar to those we find in *Dracula,* the motivation for them in the later novel is not internally justified; rather, in the second half of the novel, after the mystery has been explained, the story becomes more purely and mechanically an adventure tale, with the narrative devices serving only to provide information Stoker could not afford us any other way. As a consequence, many of the narrators we hear from briefly are incidental characters in whom the reader is interested only for the information they provide, a singularly awkward situation.

As the reader begins the novel, however, these difficulties are not initially troublesome. The first segment is a report from "The Journal of Occultism," describing the sighting of a mysterious shrouded woman afloat in a coffin in the Adriatic Sea off the coast of the Land of the Blue Mountains. Following this preface, book 1 recounts the "Reading of the Will" of one Roger Melton, followed by a report of the event—in journal form—given by one of his nephews, a greedy, transparent figure, whose role in the novel ends with the journal entry. Nevertheless, Stoker creates a voice whose truculence of tone emanating from smug self-righteousness is valuable in introducing and creating immediate reader identification with the protagonist, Rupert. Ernest Roger Halbard Melton is thus a good, though limited, foil to his cousin Rupert whose concern for his aunt, Janet MacKelpie, who raised him after his mother died, immediately endears him to us.

Through Ernest's journal, we learn that the late Roger Melton had agreed to purchase the estate of the noble Voivode (Prince) Peter Vissarion of the most noble family of the Land of the Blue Mountains, a country whose general location, physical characteristics, and history resemble those of Transylvania. The Voivode had agreed to sell his estate secretly to Melton in order to purchase the arms needed to fight the "oppressor Turks" and maintain the freedom of his country, a land threatened by the imperialism of other surrounding nations as well. The conditions of Melton's will insure the secrecy of the deal between Roger and the Voivode and require Rupert to carry out the sacred trust of aiding the brave freedom-fighters. Melton bequeaths this trust to Rupert because, having recognized Rupert's love for his aunt and having secretly followed Rupert's heroic travels and adventures throughout the world, he believes Rupert is just the man to aid the people of the Blue Mountains.

The next and major part of the novel consists of Rupert's journal and his letters to his aunt, describing his arrival in the Adriatic and some of his adventures there. One set of adventures, those in which the mystery inheres and those which Rupert conceals from his aunt, have to do with Rupert's meetings and falling in love with the lady of the shroud. Only after she and Rupert are married in a weird, nocturnal, "black mass" ceremony, does Rupert discover that his bride is not, as he had feared, a vampire, but the daughter of the Voivode Vissarion, the last male of his line, who is off in England getting help for his country—and studying the constitutional monarchy. During her father's absence, the Voivode Teuta, who has been the object of the Turkish Sultan's desires— he wishes to abduct her, marry her, and thus gain control of the Land of the Blue Mountains—appeared to die of some mysterious ailment. However, Teuta was not dead, only in a cataleptic trance, but when she awakened, those in charge determined to keep her life secret to protect her from both the Turks and her own people's doubts. The vampire story is leaked in order to allow her to take exercise at night, but she is forced to agree to wear cerements and to appear in a specially constructed boat shaped like a coffin. Thus, the mystery of her identity and nature is explained rationally, if that is the appropriate term for this plot device, and Rupert's two sets of adventures interlock at the point at which Teuta is kidnapped by the Turks.

While he has been falling in love with her at night, he has spent his days and evenings impressing and winning the trust of the Blue Mountaineers. So, when Lady Teuta is captured, Rupert becomes the leader of a small band of mountaineers at first—later of their whole army and rescue operation—and sets off to rescue from her captors the woman to whom he has been secretly married. The rescue, which turns out to be of Teuta's father as well since he returned to his country just in time to be kidnapped too, is described, point by point, in letters to Rupert's aunt who joined him at his castle shortly before he met Teuta. These letters, from various members of the local religious leadership, are written only to inform the reader of Rupert's adventures and, together with his journal entries for the same period of time, are but an awkward mechanism for getting the tale told. The rescue itself, though quite suspenseful at moments, is filled with heroics, chauvinistic confrontations between the civilized and the heathen, and "modern" machinery of war, including bullet-proof clothing, battleships, and an "aeroplane" resembling a hot-air balloon.

None of the events or tools of the rescue is as dreadful and fascinating as its counterpart in *Dracula,* though Stoker alludes to heads impaled on spiked walls reminiscent of the pleasures of Vlad the Impaler. Moreover, certain errors in dating indicate that Stoker did not expend the time and concern here that he did on some of his earlier work. The novel concludes with both father and daughter rescued in a scene characteristic of Stoker's romances, complete with the embrace among father, daughter, lover.

Characteristic, too, are the elements of the plot and narration which are most successful, those in which the mysterious and uncanny are embedded. First, is the description of Rupert's castle and its environs and of his early meetings with Teuta. After describing his own bedroom with its sliding steel shutters and its protected location in a special part of the castle, Rupert continues a letter to his aunt by portraying an ancient garden beyond his bedroom windows: the shrubs, he says, are especially light in color, and "when the moon shines . . . they all look ghastly pale. The effect is weird to the last degree, and I am sure you will enjoy it" (L, 54). This bizarre-sounding statement is clarified by the characterization of Janet MacKelpie, a woman whose fascination with the occult equals Rupert's and who is, moreover, endowed with

second sight. This component of her characterization, finally the
only supernatural element in the novel, provides for some interesting tensions and creates a number of the eerie effects of the story,
for after Rupert's clandestine though chaste meetings with Teuta
in his bedroom where the Voivoda has come for warmth and
comfort,[9] and after the marriage ceremony itself, Aunt Janet
reports dreams in which she has seen Rupert threatened by a ghostly
figure in dripping cerements. Moreover, by reading through his
Aunt Janet's books on the occult, Rupert comes to his initial and
mistaken surmise about Teuta's nature as a vampire.

As is the case throughout Stoker's fiction, many of these elements
of the uncanny belong to the Oedipal configuration of the novel's
characters. The baleful influence of Teuta described by Aunt Janet
is not the only presence felt in the early parts of the novel. Rupert
himself feels the presence of his dead mother whom he loved dearly,
who died when he was quite young, and whose approving influence
he first detects when he accepts the trust of his uncle's will and the
mission to Vissarion. Rupert repeatedly remarks that he never
thinks of his mother as dead and, indeed, analysis of the female
characters in the novel indicates that she is, on one level at least,
alive and well. First, and most obviously, is the doubling of the
mother with Aunt Janet who wishes to protect Rupert and, therefore, is initially worried and threatened by the lady of the shroud.
To comfort her, and allay her fears, Rupert plays the little boy.
His description of this scene is especially intriguing, for its autobiographical components—recall Stoker's size, for example, and
his fondness for bestowing similar dimensions on many of his
heroes—remind us that it was Charlotte Stoker who first told Bram
tales of horror and the supernatural: "Aunt Janet, old, and grey-
haired, but still retaining her girlish slimness of figure, petite,
dainty as a Dresden figure, her face lined with the care of years,
but softened and ennobled by the unselfishness of those years,
holding up my big hand, which would outweigh her whole arm;
sitting dainty as a pretty old fairy beside a recumbant giant—for
my bulk never seems so great as when I am near this real little
good fairy of my life—seven feet beside four feet seven" (L, 88).

The attraction to the little old woman requires no additional emphasis.

Moreover, Teuta herself also functions occasionally as the mother, which Rupert makes explicit in describing the events of one of their meetings: "she saw that I was moved, and tenderly stroked my hair, and with delicate touch pressed down my head on her bosom, as a mother might have done to comfort a frightened child" (*L*, 125). Earlier, anxiously and impatiently waiting to see Teuta again, he remarks: "I can only wait with what patience I can till I see her again. But to that end I can do nothing. I know absolutely nothing about her—not even her name. Patience!" (*L*, 77). This speech is rather awkwardly resonant when the reader recalls that Rupert's mother's name was Patience! When Rupert cries that he wants to keep Teuta forever, he is close to revealing to us one of the major motivating factors in Stoker's fascination with the supernatural and with vampirism: "Surely the old myths were not absolute inventions; they must have had a basis *somewhere* in fact. May not the world-old story of Orpheus and Eurydice have been based on some deep-lying principle or power of human nature? There is not one of us but has wished at some time to bring back the dead. Ay, and who has not felt that in himself or herself, was power in the deep love for our dead to make them quick again, did we but know the secret of how it was to be done?" (*L*, 97).

The explicitness of this statement, unparalleled in the other novels, and perhaps called forth by the recent death of Henry Irving as well as referring directly to the death of the woman and mother, is extremely useful in understanding the rescue motifs in all of the fiction, for to save from death is very close to recovering someone from the dead. Moreover, these rescue fantasies, as described by Freud, are often the obverse of a desire to threaten or destroy. The dream of the child or even the adult, and the fantasy of the artist, in which the loved one is placed in danger and then rescued enacts the ambivalence toward the object.[10] Hostility toward the threatened character is minimized in *The Lady of the Shroud,* though possibly still providing the motivation for the mother's being dead which otherwise seems unnecessary. Additionally, the split between a bad powerful male, the Turkish sultan, and a good powerful male, the Voivode Vissarion, also may result from a defense against ambivalence. Other of Stoker's novels express that hostility sufficiently clearly to allow us to conclude that the ambivalence is operative in this vision. Thus, *The Lady of the Shroud* reveals once again the Oedipal configuration underlying almost all of Stoker's fiction.

*The Lady of the Shroud*, then, is characteristic Stoker, with his typical plot structure, typical strengths and weaknesses. Weaker than *Dracula* and *The Jewel of Seven Stars* in terms of narration and sustaining of mystery and dread, it is finally an adventure story, its suspense depending more on the delay Rupert experiences in seeing and discovering the identity of the woman he loves and on his fear that Aunt Janet will guess what is going on, than on anything genuinely horrific in the situation. Moreover, by setting the story entirely in an exotic land, Stoker fails to exploit the terrifying juxtaposition of the bizarre and the commonplace used so effectively in *Dracula* and *Jewel*. The novel is, too, marred by the Anglo-Irish chauvinism apparent in Stoker's portrayal of the valor and nobility of the mountaineers whom he immediately places under the leadership of Rupert and his uncle, Sir Colin MacKelpie. Thus, while there is real admiration for the men of the mountains, it is cast within an imperialistic, paternalistic mold.

## The Lair of the White Worm

Stoker's last novel and, in every way his weakest, *The Lair of the White Worm*, originally published in 1911,[11] initially received favorable reviews and has been successful enough apparently to warrant reissue in 1966 and again in 1979 (though the latter publication is probably more a result of publishers capitalizing on the latest *Dracula* craze). However, it is the weakest of all his novel-length fictions, revealing impatience with plotting and characterization, inconsistency in action and tone, and a lack of overall vision or design organizing and unifying the story elements. The only real mystery of the novel concerns the motive for characters' actions. Not only does the novel fail to explain why characters respond as they do to the actions of others, but Stoker neglects to define the instigating situation in a clear, let alone credible, fashion.

Arriving for the first time in England, the protagonist, Adam Salton, an Australian, is met by his childless granduncle who intends to make Adam his heir if the younger man is suitable. The granduncle, Richard Salton, transports Adam to his home at Lesser Hill, an estate in what was once the kingdom of Mercia, where Adam meets Sir Nathaniel de Salis, Richard's oldest and most trusted friend. From here on, inexplicably, Richard Salton disappears repeatedly and most awkwardly from the action of the novel while Sir Nathaniel assumes the role of father and mentor to Adam, the men-sharing interests in geology, evolutionary history, and folklore. Apparently, Sir Nathaniel has been investigating a great mystery centered in the neighborhood, but why is never made clear. Somehow, however, the locals whom Adam meets and the actions which follow formulate the problem clearly enough for the two men to prepare for action though not clearly enough to specify the nature of the threat or the precise sort of action appropriate.

Four other characters figure in the action though each seems rather to belong to another story, an impression not at all mitigated by an awkward third-person narration which often shifts from character to character with the all-purpose transition, "meanwhile." These four characters are Edgar Caswell, last of a long line bearing the same name, cruel, dominant males of the ruling house of the region located at a place called Castra Regis. Edgar Caswell is noteworthy for his stony visage and mesmerizing stare, one he undoubtedly inherited from a precursor who worked with Mesmer himself and who "inherited" a metal trunk filled with the great hypnotist's equipment and materials which are never meaningfully employed or explained in the story. Edgar, a sort of Count Dracula manqué, then, is coming to his family seat for the first time in his adult life just as Adam arrives and the conflict between the men, explicitly described as that between evil and good, ensues as a consequence of their shared interest in two young women: one, Lilla, the granddaughter of a tenant farmer living at Mercy Farm; the other, Lilla's exotic cousin Mimi, born in Burma.

While Edgar seems attracted to Lilla and Adam to Mimi, they are locked nonetheless in a bizarre rivalry, one complicated by the fourth character, Lady Arabella March. Lady Arabella, whose husband has died recently—possibly a suicide, possibly a murder victim—requires a new husband to pay her bills, a motivation which becomes increasingly unlikely as the story progresses. Consequently, as the first lady of the land, she wishes to marry the first gentleman, Edgar Caswell. Therefore, she wishes to forestall Edgar's interest in Lilla and, to do so, conceives both an animosity toward Adam and the two young women and a plan to assist Edgar in his domination of Lilla especially (it is not clear how the latter will enable her to achieve her goals).

Lady Arabella owns and lives in a house in "Diana's Grove," probably the oldest habitation in the region, from which she can walk out in all directions, especially toward Castra Regis and Mercy Farm, and indeed is often met by Adam who also wanders around the neighborhood, checking out the folklore and local superstition he is fed by Sir Nathaniel de Salis.

The central conflict of the novel is engaged by two tenuously connected sets of events, the first, a series of bizarre tea parties at Mercy Farm at which all five principals, including Adam, are present. At these parties, for no apparent ulterior motive, Edgar Caswell attempts to hypnotize Lilla who is placed thereby under terrific emotional strain but protected by her cousin Mimi, who just as mysteriously and inexplicably possesses the force to drive Edgar back over the doorsill where, on one ludicrous occasion, he trips and falls flat on his back. On another occasion, the party resumes as if nothing untoward had occurred; indeed, in all such episodes the most fantastic fact is that everyone behaves "as usual."

The other episode defining the conflict occurs within a subplot involving Adam, Lady Arabella, and a servant of Caswell's, an African chieftain named Oolanga who has decided—not altogether off the mark—that Lady Arabella intends to steal Caswell's riches.

Suffering from delusions of grandeur, according to the other characters, Oolanga attempts to make love to Lady Arabella, hoping to join forces with her in fleecing his master. Not only does Oolanga's presence give rise to extensive racist commentary on the part of characters and narrator alike, it also provides Adam an eyewitness view of the one center of evil and mystery sustained throughout the novel: the true nature of the inhabitant of Diana's Grove. For the three characters are together one night when Lady Arabella destroys Oolanga, not by shooting him as she may have her husband, but by dragging him down with her into a deep and pestilential well-hole conveniently located in the floor of her house. As the two disappear in the foul waters, Adam recognizes that Lady Arabella is actually the white worm, or serpent, a recognition for which he has been prepared both by attacks made on her by several mongooses he carries around with him to kill the snakes which frequent the neighborhood and by her physical appearance itself. Lithe and sinuous, Lady Arabella always dresses all in white and speaks in sibilant sentences.

After telling his tale of Oolanga's demise to his mentor, and receiving in turn unconvincing—to the reader anyway—explanations of Lady Arabella's identity, of the whiteness of the worm, and of the evolutionary possibilities for the serpent, Adam vows to protect Mimi and to rid the area of the white worm forever. Conveniently, Lady Arabella offers to sell her house to Adam and, closing the deal at once though Lady Arabella does not vacate, Adam sets about filling the well-hole with alternate layers of dynamite and sand. At the same time, he has married Mimi to get her away from Mercy Farm, as a consequence of which Edgar, who is becoming increasingly demented (monomanical, Stoker would have it in a rather lengthy diagnosis in which he refers to contemporary "alienists"), has dominated Lilla into a premature grave by staring her into a faint which she does not survive. To keep himself further occupied, Edgar has been playing with a gigantic kite he runs off the tower of Castra Regis. Shaped like a hawk, the kite was originally conceived to subdue a "plague of pigeons" infesting the neighborhood. Ultimately, however, Edgar

perceives it as the visible sign of his godlike powers, and his monomanical pursuit offers Stoker the opportunity for a dénouement. As
a massive lightning storm builds, Lady Arabella incomprehensibly
albeit cooperatively attaches a metal wire to the kite and runs the
wire back to her home. When lightning strikes, both villains are
destroyed in a flash, as it were. The reader is treated to several
viewings of the remains of Lady Arabella who, as the worm, is
spewed forth from the well-hole in great white and bloody frag-
ments. As the novel ends, Adam and Mimi are off for a well-earned
honeymoon.

As is the case with the earlier horror tales, *The Lair of the White
Worm* is preoccupied with confusions of identity, extrahuman
powers, and the nature of women. Indeed, here Stoker attempted
to go further than he had elsewhere in his exploration of human
nature and history, linking human nature to the animal. Not only
is Lady Arabella possessed by both the spirit and body of a primeval
serpent, but Edgar Caswell is identified as a vulture or hawk or
other bird of prey, and thus with his kite, which threatens the
neighborhood as it soars aloft Castra Regis but remains tied to the
earthly and which is ultimately self-destructive. Moreover, Lilla and
Mimi are identified as doves, the symbol of nunnery formerly
located on the site of Mercy Farm. Lilla especially is the dove
preyed upon by hawk and serpent alike, and she dresses all in
grey just as Lady Arabella dresses all in white. Stoker's rendering
of these correspondences, however, is weak and allegorical rather
than sustained and uncanny, as similar ones are in *Dracula.* Lacking
both the extensive folklore and history underlying the earlier
novel as well as the patience with which he researched and struc-
tured *Dracula,* he was unable to make use of these motifs in any
convincing way.

While laughably bad, *The Lair of the White Worm* retains
enough of the Gothic possibilities Stoker exploited successfully
elsewhere to represent a poignant rendering of his waning interest
and powers. Indeed, so typical are the themes and so similar are
the characters to those in *Dracula* that *Worm* can serve usefully
as an introduction to Stoker's most successful work. In *Lair* good

and evil are more clearly defined provinces, but the characters manifesting one or the other resemble those in *Dracula*. The heroes and heroines include Adam, his father figure who like Van Helsing believes in the mysterious and its ultimately inexplicable yet conquerable nature, a second father figure—old Salton—who remains offstage, and the two innocent women whom the villain is attempting to conquer. As in *Dracula*, one woman is destroyed and the other marries the hero; moreover, the one who perishes seems to do so at least as much a result of her being left alone by the others as by the villain's actions—a situation we will see repeated in *Dracula*. Indeed, even the names of the heroines are similar: Lilla Watford, who dies, reminds one of Lucy Westenra, sacrificed in *Dracula*; and Mimi, of course, is Mina, each of whom is intelligent, brave, pure of heart, and the wife of the hero.

The villains in *The Lair* are less obviously reminiscent of those in *Dracula* but, as we shall see, the parallels are profound. It is here that we can begin to understand more fully both the role and nature of women in Stoker's fiction and the success of *Dracula*. In *The Lair* the existence of two villains reflects a bifurcation or diffusion of the threat and the horror: both Edgar Caswell as monomaniac and rival and Lady Arabella as primeval monster must be destroyed. Nevertheless, the threat posed by Edgar is by far the more perfunctorily and unsatisfactorily portrayed. The locus of the real horror and evil of the novel is the white worm, and on it Stoker spends far more time, explaining how Lady Arabella became the worm, or vice versa, and attempting to make the evolutionary history plausible through providing the reader the fruits of his research into the history and geology of the area. Like the sensuous vampire women of *Dracula*, Lady Arabella received a "poisonous bite" (*W*, 61) which caused her transformation; moreover, and gratuitously, she apparently attacks children, for Adam discovers in the woods the body of a child with tooth marks on its neck (*W*, 59–60). Unlike Edgar, Lady Arabella is not dismissed as insane; she remains the source of mystery and the uncanny. As is said of Adam Salton, so it is of Bram Stoker: "He was fascinated by the idea of there being a mysterious link between the woman and the animal" (W, 63), a link which Stoker both proclaimed and denied throughout his literary career, typically by splitting the woman into opposites, the all-pure (here the nun/dove) and the all evil (the sensuous serpent). We shall explore this fascination more fully in our discussion of *Dracula*.

# Chapter Five
# *Dracula*

*Dracula* (1897), Stoker's only unequivocal success, has created several subsidiary industries. In addition to the films, several of them excellent in unique ways (in particular Murnau's 1922 silent *Nosferatu,* a version of the book used without permission from Florence Stoker; the 1931 Tod Browning *Dracula* starring Bela Lugosi; the BBC made-for-television *Dracula* starring Louis Jourdan), plays, comic books, t-shirts, masks, editions of the original novel (*Dracula* has never been out of print since first issued) it has generated, it is the only fiction of Stoker's to have received any noteworthy amount of critical attention. While some of this success can be attributed to timing and shrewd entrepreneurs, the rest is due both to the considerable literary achievement of the novel and, most crucially, to the fact of the novel's sounding a near universal chord of fantasy and anxiety which has endured for over eighty years.

While Count Dracula is so familiar as to appear to need no introduction, the differences between Stoker's novel and later versions are sufficiently radical and significant that a summary of the action of *Dracula* is useful at this point. There are essentially three foci of the action in the novel: the first, that of chapters 1–4, introduces the count and Castle Dracula by taking the reader, via Jonathan Harker's journals, on a journey from the rational West to the increasingly mysterious and superstitious East of Transylvania. Harker has been sent to complete the sale to Dracula of real estate in England, but his journey is by no means ordinary. Identifying with businesslike, apparently commonsensical Harker, the reader is asked to believe the testimony of Harker's eyes as he comes to recognize Dracula for what he is, as he succumbs to

the seductiveness of the female inhabitants of the castle (the consummation is forestalled by Dracula himself—just in time), and
as he helplessly awaits what seems to be inevitable destruction. With
Harker, we learn that Dracula is making his final, painstaking arrangements to relocate his horrifying operations in England, seeking
a wider field for his deathly activities and his undead dominance of
the living.

Somehow, and the means is not clear, Harker manages to escape
Castle Dracula and, at this point, the focus shifts back to England
where we are introduced, through their correspondence, to the
heroines of the novel, Lucy Westenra and Mina Murray. While
Mina is Harker's fiancée, Lucy has achieved a triumph of sorts in
having received, in the course of one day, three proposals of marriage from three men, all friends. Dr. John Seward, the director
of an insane asylum and former student of the great and learned
Abraham Van Helsing of Amsterdam, is a moody and skeptical
representative of Western scientism. It is Seward whom Stoker
uses here as the agent for the unbelieving reader: when Van Helsing persuades Seward of the existence of vampires, he is educating
us as well. The second of Lucy's unsuccessful suitors, Quincey
Morris, is an unintentionally parodic Texan, Stoker's depiction of
the strong, chivalrous, resourceful American man of action (a trans-
planted Stoker with a terrible speech impediment). He whose
good fortune it is, or so it seems at first, to be loved and accepted
by Lucy is Arthur Holmwood, the future Lord Godalming, a
character distinguished primarily by his social class and the suffering he endures.

For while Mina and Lucy, old school friends, are corresponding
with one another, Dracula is making his inexorable way toward
the English coast. And while Lucy wishes greedily that she could
have all three men, and Mina begins to be concerned about Jonathan's long silence, Dracula approaches the coastal town of
Whitby, precisely where Lucy is vacationing with her mother.

Joined there by Mina, at which point the narrative shifts to the
women's journals, Lucy soon takes up her old restless sleepwalking.
One night an exceptionally violent storm, during which a ghostly

ship makes its way to shore, apparently without human direction, shakes the Whitby coast. When the ship runs aground we discover no living crew on board, only the captain, dead and lashed to the wheel, and a huge dog which leaps onto land and disappears. Shortly thereafter, Lucy sleepwalks to the Whitby cemetery, high atop a hill, where she is attacked on a suicide's grave by Dracula, who has made a triumphant landing on English soil, albeit in canine form.

At the same time that Lucy's sleepwalking begins, Dr. Seward has noticed increasingly restless behavior on the part of his most interesting patient, a zoophagus madman named Renfield, who collects and eats flies, spiders, birds—all the while declaiming, "The blood is the life." It is through the waxing and waning of Renfield's restlessness that the men are finally able to trace Dracula's movements in the neighborhood.

At this point, almost all the characters are introduced, as is the first stage of the plot complication. Lucy begins to report terrible dreams in which she hears the flapping of wings outside her bedroom window and from which she awakens in a state of torpor and progressive weakness. Alarmed about her, her fiancé seeks the help of Dr. Seward who calls in his old mentor, Van Helsing; it is Van Helsing's task to convince both the skeptical Seward and the incredulous reader that Lucy is suffering from the attacks of a vampire and that only certain peculiar safeguards will sustain her life. Through Van Helsing Stoker presents an encyclopedic range of vampire lore. Though their attempts to save Lucy include multiple transfusions, Lucy receiving blood from all her suitors and Van Helsing to boot, as well as the liberal use of garlic, each attempt fails in a different way and, ultimately, Lucy dies. In her final moments, Lucy reveals the essence of her vampire nature as her personality alternates between lovely maiden and the luscious voluptuary who attempts a deathbed seduction of her fiancé.

Mina, meanwhile, having received word that Jonathan is safe, though very ill and seemingly deranged, has gone to Budapest to nurse him. When they return to England, now married, the novel assumes its final focus after a last episode in the Lucy story, the famous staking scene in which, trapped in her tomb by Seward, Morris, Van Helsing, and Holmwood, Lucy, now a vampire herself, is finally laid to rest by the hand of her betrothed. We shall have more to say of this scene in another context.

Once in England, Mina becomes the new focus of attention and, after Harker has suffered the setback of glimpsing a rejuvenated Dracula in London, Mina sets to work collecting and collating the journal accounts of all the participants, thus making it possible for the men to track Dracula. When Van Helsing first meets Mina, he recognizes her as extraordinary among women, having, as he puts it, the heart of a woman and the mind of a man, and from this point the reader is not allowed to forget Mina's saintliness for a moment.

To consolidate their efforts, the characters gather at Seward's asylum where Renfield's activity provides an index of Dracula's proximity—he has purchased the castlelike estate of Carfax immediately adjacent to the asylum. When Renfield meets Mina, he, too, is immediately struck by her goodness, but, though he tries to warn the men and to protect Mina himself, it is of no avail, and Dracula enters the asylum and assaults Mina. Blind to her danger for an exasperatingly long time, Van Helsing, Seward, Morris, and Holmwood finally confront incontrovertible evidence. After they discover Renfield in his cell, dying from wounds sustained in a terrific battle with Dracula, they race up to the Harkers' room. Breaking through the door, they discover Jonathan in a trance and Mina being forced to drink Dracula's blood from a self-inflicted wound in his "bosom." In a misguided effort to innoculate Mina against further assaults, Van Helsing touches her brow with the Host. As she shrieks out in pain, the contact scorching her skin, we see the mark of Cain burned into the white skin, and Mina screams, "Unclean, unclean!" (chapter 21).

From this point, the novel approaches its resolution, as the band of rescuers, with Mina's participation now, work against the clock and the setting sun to trace and render uninhabitable Dracula's coffins, deposited around London. But Dracula himself gets away and the chase extends across the continent of Europe, requiring not only speed but ingenuity and the assistance of Mina's telepathic rapport with Dracula. (Stoker employs his knowledge of mesmerism and hypnotism in this context, with Van Helsing hypnotizing Mina so that she may report the nature of Dracula's whereabouts.) Unrelentingly suspenseful, this last section of the novel ends just at sunset and just at the door to Castle Dracula, where Quincey Morris sacrifices his life to destroy Dracula and to cleanse Mina of her stain. The others survive, however, including Jonathan who has struck the presumably fatal blow, and all live to see the birth of Mina's son, named for each member of the band of rescuers.

*Dracula* is a masterpiece of its kind not only because of the suspensefulness of this plot as outlined but because of several factors less readily reflected in a plot summary: its skillful managing and meshing of concurrent events; its focus on the reactions to Dracula of everyday people—Dracula is not "on stage" during most of the novel; its painstaking detailing not only of vampire lore, but of times and places and subordinate characters; and most crucially, its scenes of heightened horror in which the dreamlike seductiveness of the vampires is alternately langorously and pleasurably received or violently repelled. It is an extraordinarily rich novel for analysis and we shall be better equipped to undertake that analysis after discussing the literary and historical influences on Stoker, the research and method of composition he employed, and the Gothic genre of which *Dracula* is the supreme achievement.

## Sources: Historical and Literary

Stoker's sources for *Dracula*, both historical and folkloric, have been the subject of some considerable speculation, as has been the life of the historical Vlad Tepes (the Impaler) of Wallachia, presumably the prototype of the fictional Count Dracula. Fortunately, the range of speculation can be narrowed, due to a set of Stoker's notes for *Dracula* which, apparently alone among Stoker's unpublished papers, have survived for our consideration. Held by the Rosenbach Museum and Library in Philadelphia, the seventy-eight pages of notes, outlines, charts, diagrams, and clippings provide some information about both the sources and method of composition of *Dracula,* information indicating that Stoker's work on the novel was lengthy and painstaking.

With regard to folkloric sources, the information is extensive, not surprisingly reflecting Stoker's fascination with superstitions and their associated lore and rites. In addition to on location research, as it were, at Whitby, during which he collected local superstition and tales about storms, shipwrecks, and graves (and consulted coastal logbooks, meteorological manuals, and local inhabitants regarding winds, barometers, and cloud signs), Stoker read a variety of articles and books on superstition in general and Transylvanian legends and customs in particular.[1]

With regard to historical sources, the histories available to Stoker reflected confusions and inaccuracies regarding Vlad Dracula's biography, some of which persist to the present.[2] The most direct discussion of Vlad the Impaler which he seems to have read,[3] working like his character Jonathan Harker, in the British Museum, was one of the German incunabula written by Saxon merchants trading in Transylvania in the fifteenth century who suffered at the Impaler's hands and who evidently determined to expose his crimes throughout Europe. These documents included such descriptions of Vlad's atrocities as those rendered in *Dracula: A Biography of Vlad the Impaler:*

if any wife had an affair outside of marriage, Dracula ordered her sexual organs cut. She was then skinned alive and exposed in her skinless flesh in a public square, her skin hanging separately from a pole or placed on a table in the middle of the marketplace. The same punishment was applied to maidens who did not keep their virginity, and also to unchaste widows. In other instances, for similar offenses, Dracula was known to have the nipple of a woman's breast cut off. He would also have a red-hot iron stake shoved into the woman's vagina making the instrument penetrate her entrails and emerge from her mouth. He then had the woman tied to a pole naked and left her exposed there until the flesh fell from the body, and the bones detached themselves from their sockets.[4]

For a variety of reasons, including revenge against the German merchants in Transylvania who sent home the sensational accounts of his activities, Dracula violated his own trade treaties and invaded Transylvania in 1457, where he decimated the population and burned to the ground buildings and entire villages alike. His invasions into Transylvania were most extensive and horrifying during the years of 1459 and 1460:

According to the Saint Gall text, Dracula looted the Church of Saint Bartholomew, which is still in existence, "stealing the vestments and chalices." He then burned the suburb of the city located near the chapel of Saint Jacob, and impaled countless victims on the hill surrounding the chapel (Kappelenberg, Timpa Hill). It was likely on this site that Dracula is described as wining and dining among the cadavers. This episode is recalled by two famous prints, one published in 1500 at Strasburg, the other published in 1499 at Nürnberg. Both the episodes and the associated woodcuts did more to damage Dracula's reputation than any other single pamphlet or print. . . .

Dracula's vindictiveness and violence extended through the spring and summer of 1460. In the spring (April) he was finally able to catch his opponent Dan III (Danciul): he forced him to read his own funeral oration and then decapitated him—only seven of his followers were able to escape. During the summer, in early July, Dracula captured Fagaras and impaled all its citizens—men, women, and children —states the Saint Gall manuscript. One month later—the German narration specifies "on the day of Saint Bartholomew," August 24, 1460—Dracula raided the town of "Humilasch," evidently Amlas, and burned it, impaling all its citizens, with the priest leading the procession, a belated revenge for its continued defiance since 1456. Although statistics are very difficult to establish, particularly for that period (and the German figures must be viewed with caution), there were more victims on the night of Saint Bartholomew in 1460, in the town of Amlas—twenty thousand may have perished—than were butchered by Catherine de Médicis in Paris over a century later.[5]

In sum, it has been estimated that Dracula murdered between forty and one hundred thousand men, women, and children during the six years of his second reign, his acts of cruelty possibly providing a model for Ivan the Terrible.

Stoker's notes indicate his familiarity with some of the lore surrounding the historical figure as well; for example, he observes one of several meanings of "Dracula," a name referring also to the Order of the Dragon to which Dracula, like his father, belonged: "Dracula in Wallachian means Devil. Wallachians were accustomed to give it as a surname to any person who rendered himself conspicuous by courage, cruel actions or cunning."[6]

Thus, from Dracula, the Impaler whose greatest pleasure derived from the prolonged draining of his victims' blood, through dragon, to Devil, to the vampire was not a very long stretch of the imagination, though Stoker may have been the first to make the connection.

Moreover, even a cursory consideration of both the literary and contemporary topical sources suggests that Stoker's conflation of the figure of the vampire, known to the English originally through eighteenth-century travelers' accounts of vampire scares in Eastern Europe, especially in Hungary,[7] with the historical Dracula was logical. To mention first those related contemporary events which must have made Stoker even more receptive to the literary influences, we can follow the suggestion of the biographers of Vlad Dracula and recall the horror of Jack the Ripper in London; the translation by Sir Richard Burton, whom Stoker knew personally, of twenty-five tales about a vampire written centuries before by the Indian sage Bhavabhuti; the publication of Frazer's *The Golden Bough* which detailed vampire superstitions, and Stoker's membership in an occult lodge called "Golden Dawn in the Outer" to which Montague Summers also belonged.[8]

Most directly in the literary tradition, however, are a group of tales typically viewed as influencing Stoker. In particular, *The Vampyre, A Tale* (1819) by Dr. John Polidori (by some confusion originally attributed to Lord Byron whose traveling companion Polidori was in 1816 and who evidently outlined the plot which Polidori elaborated), a brief rendering of a young Englishman's fascination with a Count Ruthven whom he sees first at a party in London and with whom he then travels across Europe to Italy and Greece (very much like Byron and Polidori—indeed the story qualifies as a *roman à clef*). Somewhat alarmed by tales of women gone wild after vaguely suggested intimacy with the count, and of those destroyed after sitting at the gaming table with him, the hero dismisses his suspicions of Ruthven after the count nurses him tenderly back to health; this despite the fact that Aubrey, the hero, has fallen ill in response to Ruthven's destruction of two maidens, one Italian and one Greek.

While they are still in Greece, Count Ruthven begins himself to weaken and, indeed, seems to be dying. Exacting a promise from Aubrey that he will not say a word about Ruthven until a year and a day have passed, the count, having insured also that his body will be placed in the moonlight, appears to expire. Having sworn himself to silence, Aubrey soon watches helplessly and is driven to the brink of madness as a resurrected Ruthven returns to England to woo, seduce, and destroy the hero's own sister.

Decidedly pale in the light of *Dracula, The Vampyre, A Tale* prefigures the cold, aristocratic fascination exercised by Count Dracula (and exaggerated in the stage and film versions). Count Ruthven is, of course, quite literally Byronic in Polidori's depiction, the two traveling companions having found their relations strained almost as soon as they set out. Only at the very end of the tale, however, and for only a moment or two, is there a suggestion of the suspensefulness possible in the vampire tale and fully realized in Stoker's achievement.

What is in some ways more interesting is that, traveling with Byron, Polidori was one of the famous company which gathered together one rainy night in the summer of 1816 in Switzerland and determined that each should write a horror story. The only other tale to result from that night's conversation was, of course, Mary Shelley's *Frankenstein,* to which Dracula bears a family resemblance. Noteworthy among the similarities are the structure of multiple narration (which we will discuss again later), the suspenseful final chase across a continent, the concern with transcending the limits of the scientifically possible, with transgressing the boundary between life and death, the ambivalence toward female characters set in the context of incest, an interest in dreams, and the portrayal of the monster as dignified and pitiable, a state achieved by Dracula only once or twice, when he describes his heritage to Harker and when Mina expresses pity for him.

The juxtaposition of Polidori's tale, Shelley's superb novel, and Stoker's supreme Gothic fiction foregrounds the villain as a Faustian Wandering Jew, a Prometheus, the Byronic hero—archetype of so many romantic fictions and narrative poems. In *Frankenstein,* he is the overreaching intellectual, the Faust, or the "modern Prometheus," as Shelley herself suggests to us in the subtitle. In *Dracula* as well the villain descends from the Wandering Jew; like the Wandering Jew, Dracula cannot die and "speaks of nations long extinct as though personally acquainted with them." Like his biblical prototype, his immortality is, in one sense, a punishment and a torment. However, like Faust, Dracula not only could not die, he would not die. Thus, the fusion of the Faust myth with the legend of the Wandering Jew "give[s] rise to the legend of the exchange of eternal bliss for everlasting life and happiness on earth. . . ."[9]

In his discussion of this fusion of myths in the context of Matthew Lewis's *The Monk,* Eino Railo says, "As Lewis's own contribution I am inclined to regard the Jew's large, black, flashing eyes, whose glance awakened horror, his melancholy and his noble majesty. . . . The latter half of the eighteenth century was the heyday of Mesmerism, at a time when 'animal magnetism' and quackery based on that idea were extremely fashionable; the species of 'magnetism' which flowed, according to Mesmer, from the human eye, in other words, the hypnotic power of the eye was adopted by the romanticists to serve their own purposes. . . ."[10]

A number of themes converge in the image of the hypnotic eye, themes Stoker was preoccupied with throughout his life. Certainly, the reader of *Dracula* cannot forget the vampires' ability to hypnotize and to communicate telepathically; additionally, we will recall the cataleptic trances of Mr. Trelawny and Nurse Kennedy in *The Jewel of Seven Stars* and of Teuta in *The Lady of the Shroud* and the mesmerizing gaze of Edgar Caswell in *The Lair of the*

*White Worm.* In his notes for *Dracula,* Stoker includes a reference to *"The Theory of Dreams,* 2 vols. F. C. & J. Rivington 62 St. Paul's Churchyds 1808," from which he noted the "oddness of the sleep state" and cited a case of a woman who endured cataleptic trances twice daily. His *Famous Imposters* included a chapter on Mesmer himself.

However, the fusion of the Faust and Wandering Jew legends has had a greater influence on the more recent depictions of Dracula than on *Dracula* itself, for Stoker's modern Prometheus is, as we shall see, both far less the tragically heroic overreacher, and in fact far less the focus of the tale, than his counterparts in romantic fiction and poetry and in contemporary film.

The third work often cited as influential for Stoker can be used to clarify and introduce an analysis of this different emphasis of Stoker's novel. Joseph Sheridan Le Fanu's *Carmilla* (1871) can be linked directly to Stoker's *Dracula,* for it is demonstrably the precursor to a chapter excised from the final version of the novel, a chapter entitled "Dracula's Guest." Indeed, Transylvania was not the original location of Castle Dracula; rather, that replaces "Styria" in the notes, a name which Stoker lifted from *Carmilla.*

In Le Fanu's tale, one of the stories collected in *In a Glass Darkly* (loosely linked together as the collected papers of one Doctor Hesselius), the vampire Carmilla, in earlier manifestations known as Mircalla and Millarca, the Countess Karnstein, preys on a succession of lovely maidens, the last of whom has been saved just in time and who lives to narrate her tale. The attacks on the maidens, which are identical to one another from the introduction of the vampire to the young girl and her father, to her engaging their protection, to her assault on the maiden, are extremely erotic, fascinating yet repellent. Carmilla croons to the narrator, for instance, "In the rapture of my enormous humiliation I live in your warm life, and you shall die—die, sweetly die—into mine. I cannot help it; as I draw near to you, you, in your turn will draw near to others, and learn the rapture of that cruelty, which yet is love. . . ."[11] The narrator, upon such occasions, becomes literally entranced. "I experienced a strange tumultuous excitement that was pleasurable, ever and anon, mingled with a vague sense of fear and disgust."

At the end of the story we learn that Mircalla, Countess Karnstein of Styria, had become a vampire by suffering the bite of one who had committed suicide. This information, and the subsequent trial and staking of the vampire in her tomb, is afforded through the offices of one Baron Vordenburg who lives in a town called Gratz. The narrator's tale ends rather hauntingly as, even after the presumed destruction of the countess, she reports "often from a reverie I have started, fancying I heard the light step of Carmilla at the drawing-room door."[12]

In "Dracula's Guest," Stoker incorporates some few details, mainly the names Styria and Gratz and the idea of a vampire countess who herself, in this case, committed suicide. He was also undoubtedly impressed by the female eroticism Le Fanu evokes, though as Mario Praz describes the tradition in *The Romantic Agony*, the image of the fatal woman was available to Stoker from many other sources.[13] Nonetheless, the focus in *Carmilla* exclusively on female vampirism provides an important key to the emphasis in Stoker's novel.

"Dracula's Guest"[14] concerns an episode occurring during Jonathan Harker's journey to Castle Dracula (though Harker is not named here) when, stopping over at Munich, Harker takes a side trip into the country only a few hours before Walpurgisnacht. Warned by both the innkeeper and coachman of the dangers he risks, Harker inexplicably and obstinately leaves the wiser coachman and wanders off to a deserted village (resembling the desolate home town of the countess in *Carmilla*) just as a brutal snow storm approaches. Lost in the storm, Harker stumbles into a cemetery where he seeks shelter in the doorway of the mausoleum of "Countess Dolingen of Gratz in Styria [who] sought and found death 1801." Oddly, the tomb is distinguished by a huge metal stake driven through it. In a flash of lightning, the hero sees "as my eyes were turned into the darkness of the tomb, a beautiful woman, with rounded cheeks and red lips, seemingly asleep on a bier." Another flash of lightning strikes the stake and, we are to assume, destroys the vampire who shrieks hideously.

The most uncanny element of the tale, however, concerns the protection from both the countess and the storm Harker is provided by an unrecognized force—undoubtedly Dracula himself. This force first pulls Harker from the tomb, then, as a wolf, lies on Harker to keep him from freezing—meanwhile, taking some nourishment at the hero's throat—then yelps helpfully, enabling the soldiers who have been sent on the rescue mission to locate the unconscious Harker. At the end of the story, we discover that the rescue was masterminded by Dracula.

Thus, "Dracula's Guest," and its relation to *Carmilla,* is interesting for two reasons. First, it indicates a shift in focus from the Promethean overreacher type of villain (or vampire) to the insidiously seductive female, as we shall see even more clearly in our analysis of *Dracula.* Second, it is revealing in a study of *Dracula*'s composition: clearly unmotivated and redundant in part with scenes surviving in the novel, this tale was rightly deleted by Stoker.

## The Composition of *Dracula*

Given both the bloody atrocities of the reign of Vlad the Impaler and the vampire tradition in nineteenth-century fiction, one cannot be surprised that Stoker chose to make the architect of Castle Dracula into a vampire count. The documents at the Rosenbach not only reflect both the historic and folklore components which Stoker fused in creating the figure of Dracula, but also provide invaluable information regarding Stoker's method of composition for this novel—and, in fact, for one other we will examine shortly, *The Mystery of the Sea.*

As we have seen, in research beginning in early 1890,[15] Stoker consulted coastguard logbooks and local folklore on ship sailings and wrecks, had conversations with residents and walked through the Whitby churchyard where he saw the grave of one Ann Swales (recall old Mr. Swales in *Dracula*), read articles concerning vampire reports in New England, studied clothing, agricultural, and culinary fashions as well as vampire lore of the Carpathians, made diagrams and sketches of views from various locations at Whitby, and consulted manuals about barometers, wind shifts, cyclones, cloud signs, paying particular attention to correlations among various winds, storms, clouds. It is likely, further, that he carried on his research and the composition of *Dracula* in a peripatetic fashion, since the slips of paper on which the notes appear are various, ranging from account sheets to hotel stationery ("The Stratford" in Philadelphia) to Lyceum Theater paper. Moreover, he consulted his brother, "Sir Wm. Thornley Stoker, Bart., Pres., Royal College of Surgeons, Eng.," for the precise description of what would be the symptoms and treatment of an injury to one side of the head above the ear. The surgeon replied: "Trephining to remove the depressed bone, or to give the surgeon opportunity to remove the blood clot might give instant relief. I have seen a patient in profound coma, begin to move his limbs and curse and swear during the operation. The more recent the injury, the more rapid the relief. A patient dying of these conditions would be profoundly comotose, and stertorous in his breathing." Thus Stoker received the information he required to describe exactly Renfield's last moments.

Finally, as he blocked out the novel in draft, we can observe a number of details regarding what might have been a typical *modus operandi,* but probably was not in some of the weaker fictional work. From the first, Stoker seems to have had a relatively clear conception of the general pattern the book was to follow. This pattern was rather complicated and Stoker was aware from the outset of the need to date very carefully events and the letters, journals, or diaries in which they are reported. He was clearly working with a calendar in front of him and, though he slips occasionally on a date for a report or an incident, the rest is sufficiently accurate to enable us to locate and correct the error. Several of the note pages contain dates the events for which were never filled in, so it is likely that Stoker set out the calendar first. Moreover, on a piece of Lyceum Theater paper, dated 14 March 1890, Stoker blocked out four books of *Dracula,* each including seven chapters. (The magic number seven again, though later he replaced this scheme with one of nine chapters per book; it is impossible to tell when Stoker finally discarded this scheme of numbering altogether.) The chapter headings, primarily those in book 2, are emended and, since this book concerns the Whitby episodes, we might conclude that the emendations were based on research done at the site later that year.

Additionally, in the original planning, though the trip of Harker to Transylvania and the role of Dr. Seward in book 1 seem the same as in the final version, in book 3 the Texan was going to be sent to Transylvania. Perhaps this journey was to coincide with Dracula's coming to England and was therefore finally determined to be a superfluous wild vampire chase. In any event, in the margin for book 4 is what appears to be a later note: "bring in the Texan."

The four books listed here, labeled in order, "to London" (including Harker's visit to Castle Dracula), "Tragedy" (the Whitby section), "Discovery" (referring presumably to Dracula located in London in the seventh chapter), and "Punishment" (the sixth chapter of which returns the cast to Transylvania), reflect a conscious plan for sustaining suspense, the last chapter of each book deepening the mystery while climaxing a section of the plot (the mystery of Renfield, the destruction of Lucy in her tomb, the discovery of Dracula in London, and the finale, respectively).

Following this sheet in the papers at the Rosenbach are a series of pages for more detailed outlines of the chapters. While the notes on these pages are sketchy in some cases, clearly identifiable are, for instance, the scenes describing the vampire women at the castle; a visit Lucy pays to Seward's asylum and to his patient Renfield (in the final version it is Mina who makes this visit), and the scenes describing Lucy's "seduction" by Dracula when she is at Whitby and her subsequent weakening and death. The notes for book 3 are full and quite close to the final version and include no reference to the Texan going to Transylvania, so we may conclude that they are, at the earliest, contemporaneous with

the revisions of the first outline. The notes for book 4, however, are most confusing. Lucy seems to be alive still and unfamiliar
characters and episodes are sketchily blocked in. What does seem
clear is that Stoker did not originally plan for Dracula to attack
Mina also; rather, Mina, some of whose story is outlined on
separate sheets, replaced Lucy once Stoker recognized he had
to kill (or had already killed) Lucy off earlier. Thus, the argument that Lucy and Mina are doubles, an argument which we will
advance, is strengthened by the evidence of these notes. The set
of notes is incomplete, however, and no further revisions seem
to have survived.

Evidently, Stoker began with a larger cast of characters and
number of episodes than remain in the final version. Not only
did he excise "Dracula's Guest," but there are notes for scenes
in a Munich "death-house" and for a dinner party for thirteen
guests at the end of which the count was to appear, neither of
which finally made their way into the novel. As we have seen
elsewhere, Stoker's tendency was to employ more characters than
are justified by the texts, but in *Dracula* he was able to reduce
the number to those for whom there is some justification—and those
for whom no obvious narrative justification exists (like Lord
Godalming's father, for example), may be explained in psychological terms. Moreover, the final names of the characters were only
arrived at gradually, with Stoker crossing out earlier possibilities
as he reconsidered. Indeed, on one such list, labeled "Historiae
Personae Dracula," appears the following: "The Count—Count
Vampry [crossed out] Dracula [substituted]." Some of the additional deletions and substitutions are also of interest: Quincey
Morris, the Texan, apparently derives from two characters in the
notes, "An American Inventor from Texas" (crossed out) and "A
Texan—Brutus M. Moris." One can speculate that Stoker changed
his mind about the quite wonderful "Brutus" because its suggestion of almost fraternal betrayal was dissonant with the tone
of sibling affection he wished to create. In addition to "a German
Professor—Max Windsfoeffel" (the spelling is questionable) we
also find "A Detective" and "A Psychical Research Agent—Alfred

Singleton"; most amusingly, Stoker lists "A Deaf Mute Woman" and "A Silent Man" as "English Servants of the Count." Judging from the nature of the deletion marks Stoker used, it is possible to argue that he did not relinquish all these characters at once.

Thus, the material in the Rosenbach tells us that Stoker worked thoughtfully and carefully, for a period exceeding six years, during which time he reconsidered characters, scenes, and organization.

### The Mystery of the Sea

While working on Dracula during Cruden Bay holidays—or immediately after completing it, Stoker was evidently also writing *The Mystery of the Sea,* first published in 1902.[16] In terms of plotting, scenic description, and the careful synchronizing of events and correlating of narrative elements, *The Mystery of the Sea* is as carefully constructed as *Dracula.* A consideration of the later novel in this context will be helpful in distinguishing those elements of *Dracula* which account for its enduring appeal, for, in many ways, *The Mystery of the Sea* is as strong and, indeed, a more mature work; yet it has passed into obscurity while *Dracula* survives.

The reader of both novels, armed with the information afforded by Stoker's notes for *Dracula,* can envision Stoker working in a similar way preparing the later novel, for *Mystery* reveals the same attention to detail and setting, similar fictionalizing of historical events, and the same goal of achieving a precise convergence of narrative threads.

Finally, *Mystery* is a sort of compendium of themes and narrative techniques Stoker worked with elsewhere in his fiction: like *The Jewel of Seven Stars, The Mystery of the Sea* employs a first-person narrator who is the hero of the tale and who brings to light various secret historical events which come to a crisis in the present; as is the case in *The Lady of the Shroud,* there is a subordinate character in *Mystery* who has second sight, but here the hero shares this gift; like *The Snake's Pass, Mystery* entails the discovery of a treasure hidden by the enemies of England, this time the Spanish of the Armada, a treasure identified here, too, with the heroine of the story. The heroine of this novel, Marjory Anita Drake, descendant of Sir Francis Drake, and a great American heiress and patriot, manifests the same dual nature of the ideal woman as analyzed by Stoker in *The Man:* she is gentle and self-sacrificing, on the one hand, and independent, brave, and strong, on the other. Unlike Mina Harker, however, she is distinctly sensual, though in his typical Victorian fashion, Stoker presents the male character as sexually eager and the female as sexually dutiful.

The plot of *Mystery* is a familiar one: it concerns the discovery of a great treasure, entrusted by the pope (the novel is rather strikingly anti-Catholic in perspective) to one Bernardino de Escoban, an officer of the Spanish Armada, which treasure was to be used to overthrow the power of the Anglican Church in England and which, it turns out, was hidden in a cave directly and conveniently located under a house the hero, Archie Hunter, is building at Cruden Bay. Archie learns of the treasure by decoding the Baconian cipher de Escoban used to explain the family trust to his descendants after his own mission failed. Simultaneous with his early and presumably fated discovery of the papers in which the cipher was included, Archie meets and falls in love with Marjory (when he rescues her from a rising tide) who, because she is so rich, is in hiding from a plethora of greedy suitors. Marjory returns Archie's love, they are secretly married, and together they attempt to recover the treasure.

Set during the Spanish American War, the story is complicated by two factors. The American government, aware that a conspiracy exists on the part of the dastardly Spanish to abduct Marjory, the emblem of American patriotism (she has given a fully equipped battleship to her government), attempts to provide her with unsolicited and undesired protection. And, the present descendant of Bernardino de Escoban, who is introduced as the owner of the house Marjory has chosen for her hideaway, is on the trail of the treasure.

Once Marjory is abducted, however, the present de Escoban, as a true gentleman, decides the honor of a woman is an overriding consideration. Winning the hero's grudging respect, he is, nevertheless, killed while assisting in the rescue, one resembling that in several other novels, in which a band of gallant men saves the heroine in the nick of time.

While weakened by excessive narrative sentimentalizing and editorializing regarding the wonders of a true and good woman, by gratuitous and rather violent racism, and by some incredible footwork by which Marjory employs the cipher to inform Archie of her whereabouts as she is being abducted, *The Mystery of the Sea* is nevertheless compelling reading. Enhanced by some excellent descriptions of the Cruden Bay area, which Stoker knew well, the plot, though based on coincidence, unravels with a sort of fated inevitability. Indeed, since the novel begins with an excellent exposition in which Archie comes to recognize mysterious forces, inexplicable yet operative, all around him, the reader is asked to accept, not coincidence, but the Fates. Once this is achieved through Archie's acceptance, the plot is perfectly credible.

The conclusion of *The Mystery of the Sea* is rather uncharacteristic for Stoker. With the rescue of Marjory, the death of de Escoban, and the routing of the villains, no further mention is made of the treasure which, presumably, has sunk, along with its ignominious purpose, to the bottom of the sea. Nor is there any final sentimentalizing of the relationship between Archie and Marjory. Indeed, the love story here is in several regards uncharacteristic: there is no Oedipal rivalry, no father figure, and no ambivalence toward the female. Moreover, the hero and heroine are married, if only in name, through much of the novel, and they function as equal partners. There is, thus, a restraint and maturity about this novel that is both atypical for Stoker and the signal of a greater achievement than that of many of his other tales. While we recognize the usual autobiographical projections onto the hero who, like Stoker, though an invalid as a child, is a massive, athletic adult and who has tremendous respect for the United States, we can also appreciate the unusually skillful rendering of dialect spoken by those whose native tongue is Gaelic. Moreover, the sensitivity of hero toward heroine is far more delicate and truly respectful, bespeaking greater character complexity, than is the case elsewhere in the fiction we have examined. Consequently, although *The Mystery of the Sea* belongs with other Stoker romance/adventures, it is an unusually strong and mature production which, by virtue of what it is not in Stoker's canon—despite the use of the supernatural in the ideas of the Fates and of second sight, this is by no means a Gothic novel—clarifies the nature and successful appeal of *Dracula,* the supreme embodiment of Gothic themes and techniques.

## *Dracula* as Gothic Fiction

*Dracula* exerts a complex fascination owing both to Stoker's skill and to the enduring appeal of the Gothic genre of which it is a superb and instructive example, following a tradition originated, by critical consensus, by Horace Walpole with his *Castle of Otranto* (1764). The most commonly cited pillars of the tradition are William Beckford's *Vathek* (1786), Ann Radcliffe's *The Mysteries of Udolpho* (1794) and *The Italian* (1797), Matthew Lewis's *The Monk* (1796), Mary Shelley's *Frankenstein* (1818), and Charles Maturin's *Melmoth the Wanderer* (1820).

While Stoker's themes and techniques in *Dracula* resemble those appearing in his other fictional works, only in several of the short tales and *Dracula* did he write true Gothic fiction, as superbly defined in a recent study by Elizabeth MacAndrew:

The later authors added new devices to fit their particular needs but all these works are set up as revelations of horror. They present as psychological evil a sexual obsession, overwhelming guilt, or pride that defies the limits God has set for man, and they seek to arouse fear and sickening horror in the reader. These tales may see evil as an aberration of man or as an inherent part of his nature, they may question the value judgments placed on the phenomena they are symbolizing, but they all show the world its own dreams, drawing the reader into their closed worlds, playing on his emotions, and preventing him from denying that what he experiences in the novel may also be within himself.[17]

Moreover, and especially later in the nineteenth century, Gothic fiction is increasingly dreamlike in ambience, if not explicitly entailing a dream or dreams, and symbolic in import. As we have seen, Stoker is fascinated by dreams and dreamlike states, such as hypnotic trances and catalepsy. Throughout *Dracula*, the manifestations of the vampire occur in dreams or produce trances.

The cause of the increasing emphasis on dreams in the fiction of the second half of the nineteenth century lies in the changing views of the human psyche, and the function of the dream and other typical devices of the Gothic is to indicate to the reader that the Gothic occurrences are externalized, "quasi-allegorical" representations of internal conflict: "increasingly writers chose the Gothic tale as a vehicle for ideas about psychological evil—evil not as a force exterior to man, but as a distortion, a warping of his mind." Thus, the Gothic originated late in the eighteenth century as a moral tale directing readers to eschew the evil which, though external, threatened them, but developed by the end of the nineteenth century into a psychologically more complex mode with "ambiguous presentations that questioned the nature of evil itself."[18]

MacAndrew's argument that the Gothic tale is to be taken symbolically is illuminating, too, with regard to typical Gothic devices. The castle, in particular, perhaps the preeminent emblem of the Gothic[19] and its typically alien and exotic location, is the domain not only of the villain, but of a certain mode of behavior or manifestation of self: entered by hero and/or heroine, it is the locus of trials which, in the best fiction, represent maturing lessons for them. (This is especially clear in the novels of Ann Radcliffe and in Jane Austen's parody of the genre, *Northanger Abbey*; one can also argue that Emily Brontë uses Wuthering Heights in a similar fashion.) Thus, the castle and related structures—in *Dracula,* there are three such edifices, all important, the Castle Dracula itself, Carfax in London, and its nearest neighbor, the lunatic asylum—are visual emblems of mental aberrations, transformations, and tests, the symbolic force of which may help to explain their appeal and threat.[20]

The apparently archetypal vision of Castle Dracula, although more implied than explicitly described, which the reader glimpses as Harker is first swept to his destination, is itself suggestive, not only of the exotic and isolated, but also of the terrifying interior of the grave (rife with the sickeningly corrupt odor of fleshly dissolution) and of the hauntingly familiar face of the mother, as we shall see. Thus, the castle itself is the visible and uncanny emblem of that which is repressed.[21]

Seward's asylum is equally suggestive, for when Dracula's attacks on Mina begin, we are continuously reminded that Renfield, who attempts to fight his "Master" to save her soul, is locked in a cell in a lower part of the building analogous to the "lower" impulses in the psyche. Thus, the asylum is the arena for a *psychomachia* in which the madman is simultaneously the locus of the edifice's vulnerability (Dracula enters at Renfield's invitation) and the most clear-sighted of all the men wishing to protect Mina. This is an especially vivid example both of the ambivalence of the male characters toward the female and of the symbolic significance of the Gothic edifice.

Reinforcing the symbolic rendering of the castle, the magical spaces of the Gothic are frequently hung with mirrors or fraught with various reflecting devices. Mirrors are a central metaphor for the self and, certainly, their near-universal appearance in doppelgänger tales (tales involving characters who double for each other, who split into or are multiplied by either identical or complementary characters) confirms this. Most enigmatically and terrifyingly in the vampire tale is, of course, the "fact" that a vampire does not cast a reflection, being "undead," soulless. "In Stoker's fiction . . . the invisibility of the vampire [in the mirror] serves the larger Christian allegory [of the presence or absence of souls] by emphasizing that we cannot see vampires because (a) we tend not to believe in them and (b) we choose not to see those aspects of *ourselves* that are most likely those of the vampire."[22] Thus, vampires may strike with even less warning than other ghouls or revenants.

In addition to the use of the castle, dungeon, or cave as

magical spaces which exacerbate terror, writers of Gothic tales employ narrative devices which enhance both the mystery and suspense and the sense of an alien world. MacAndrew remarks that the technique of multiple narration mediates between the reader and the mysterious space, especially when the several narrators are separated by large spans of time as well as by space. But "when the tale is no longer set in the distant past, a system of 'nested,' concentric narration maintains the illusion of a strange world, isolating a symbolic landscape within the ordinary 'world.' "[23] Additionally, as in *Dracula,* those to whom letters are being addressed while initially safely separated from the alien world, are often increasingly drawn in, and so, with delighted discomfort, is the reader. In *Dracula,* while the dialogue of the characters is frequently and distractingly laughable—notably that of Quincey Morris, the Texan, and Abraham Van Helsing, the Dutchman— Stoker achieves remarkable success in sustaining suspense by careful pacing of disclosures and painstaking collating of evidence individually collected, what MacAndrew refers to as a cumulative technique employed not only by earlier writers of the Gothic, but also by practitioners of detective fiction which was an established subgenre before 1897.

Thus, the alien worlds of the Gothic are clearly demarcated from the ordinary world by a number of techniques, and this delineation of boundaries reinforces the symbolic import of the tale. We recall from *The Jewel of the Seven Stars,* Stoker's careful and evocative use of space and the labyrinthine path to the cave followed by the initiates, duplicating Trelawny's earlier journeys to Queen Tera's rock-tomb in Egypt. In *The Lady of the Shroud,* Stoker once again employs Transylvania as the exotic land, but neither Rupert's castle nor the twist the plot takes is calculated to sustain the symbolic or the suspense. For unlike the developments in *Dracula,* the rational West invades the mysterious East, de-mystifying both the East and what terror the story began with.

In *Dracula,* however, Stoker was able to sustain the Gothic mood and symbolism, indeed, to achieve terrifying effects by bringing the world of Castle Dracula into contemporary London.

Jonathan Harker, we recall, is driven almost mad when he first catches sight of Dracula on the streets of London. This politically and racially chauvinistic equation of evil and irrationality with the East and virtue and sanity with the West[24] breaks down, however, in a number of ways. Not only does Van Helsing speak to his former pupil, Dr. Seward, of the necessity for recognizing the existence of seemingly unnatural phenomena, but the evil that is Dracula invades far more than just England itself. While it is unclear to what extent Stoker was aware that his vampire represents the evil or repressed fantasies of his characters, it is the case that the associations of violence with madness and vampirism with sexuality are typical in the Gothic. True to the nature of the Gothic, Dracula is the external representation of Renfield's insanity, Lucy and Mina's sexuality, and Harker's episodes both of delirium and passivity.

By setting part of *Dracula* in a lunatic asylum and including doctors of the human psyche as two of the major characters, Stoker gives additional evidence of his continued interest in unconscious forces and provides further corroboration of his conscious psychological speculations. And, with his interest in the fusing of identities, an interest relevant also to his appreciation of Henry Irving's ability utterly to transform himself into his roles, it is impossible that Stoker was unaware of some of the ways in which *Dracula* is a projection of the characters in the novel. Moreover, *Dr. Jekyll and Mr. Hyde* had been published in 1886, and from at least as far back as *Frankenstein* the "monster" is portrayed as the double of the hero. In choosing to write of vampires, Stoker chose a creature which is "in origin the human victim of another vampire."[25] Dracula is a true Gothic villain, "a mythic, symbolic figure. He is presented through techniques that show, not frail humans, but the nature of human frailty. These villains are symbolically . . . diabolical, and they appear along with ghosts and monsters to reproduce evil, madness, and torment located in the human mind. Their vices are presented as distortions of human nature and as essentially unnatural."[26]

Thus, characterization in *Dracula* is typical of the Gothic genre in the Victorian Era if not before. Dramatizing the theme that external horrors are manifestations of internal states, character doublings and splittings abound. While the most obvious examples of this technique are the splitting of Lucy into pure maiden and vampire, and the doubling of Van Helsing, the leader of the virtuous, for Dracula, the king of the undead, other doublings and fusions of character are equally significant. Indeed, doublings and splittings as a technique of both characterization and thematic dramatization are critical to *Dracula* as a Gothic fiction and to an understanding of the fantasy's import.

## Stoker's Vampires[27]

Bram Stoker's *Dracula* is an enduring success "not merely because it has been skillfully marketed by entrepreneurs but because it expresses something that large numbers of readers feel to be true about their own lives."[28] In other words, *Dracula* successfully manages a fantasy which is congruent with a fundamental fantasy shared by many others. This "core fantasy"[29] appears to derive from the Oedipus complex—indeed, *Dracula* has been seen as "a quite blatant demonstration of the Oedipus complex . . . a kind of incestuous, necrophilous, oral-anal-sadistic all-in wrestling match."[30]

Nevertheless, the exploration of an Oedipal conflict does not go far enough in explaining the novel: in explaining the primary focus of the fantasy content and in explaining what allows Stoker and, vicariously, his readers, to act out what are essentially threatening, even horrifying wishes which must engage the most polarized of ambivalences.

In the following, we will argue that the primary source of the ambivalences and fantasies in *Dracula* is pre-Oedipal, alternately focusing on "morbid dread"[31] and lustful anticipation of an oral fusion with the mother. For both the Victorians and twentieth-century readers, much of the novel's great appeal derives from its ambivalence toward female sexuality, a recurrent theme in Stoker's fiction, as we have seen. In *Dracula* the polarization of responses toward women characters receives its definitive embodiment, manifested both in the conflicting attitudes of the male characters and explicitly in the portrayals of the females.

The ambivalence toward female sexuality is dramatized in a series of thematically interlocking scenes, scenes portraying heightened female sexuality in all its oral seductiveness and, in reaction, scenes depicting extraordinary phallic violence. The most striking instances of the ambivalent attitude and its attendant imagery include, first, the scene in which, searching Castle Dracula in a state of fascinated dread for proof of his host's nature, Harker is greeted by three vampire women whose relation to Dracula is incestuous[32] and whose appeal is described almost pornographically: "All three had brilliant white teeth that shone like pearls against the ruby of their voluptuous lips. There was something about them that made me uneasy, some longing and at the same time deadly fear. I felt in my heart a wicked, burning desire that they would kiss me with those red lips." The three debate who has the right to feast on Jonathan first, but they conclude, "He is young and strong; there are kisses for us all," Jonathan meanwhile experiencing "an agony of delightful anticipation" (Chapter 3). At the very end of the novel, Van Helsing falls prey to the same attempted seduction by, and the same ambivalence toward, the three vampires.

Two more scenes of relatively explicit and uninhibited oral and phallic sexuality mark the novel about one half, then two thirds, through. First the scene in which Lucy Westenra is laid to her final rest by her fiancé, Arthur Holmwood, later Lord Godalming. which is worth quoting from at length:

Arthur placed the point [of the stake] over the heart, and as I looked I could see its dint in the white flesh. Then he struck with all his might.

The thing in the coffin writhed: and a hideous, blood-curdling screech came from the opened red lips. The body shook and quivered and twisted in wild contortions; the sharp white teeth champed together till the lips were cut, and the mouth was smeared with a crimson foam. But Arthur never faltered. He looked like a figure of Thor as his untrembling arm rose and fell, driving deeper and deeper the mercy-bearing stake, whilst the blood from the pierced heart welled and spurted up around it (Chapter 16).

Finally, we recall the scene which Joseph Bierman has described quite correctly as a "primal scene in oral terms,"[33] the scene in which Dracula slits open his breast and forces Mina Harker to drink his blood: "With his left hand he held both Mrs. Harker's hands, keeping them away with her arms at full tension; his right hand gripped her by the back of the neck, forcing her face down on his bosom. Her white nightdress was smeared with blood, and a thin stream trickled down the man's bare chest which was shown by his torn-open dress. The attitude of the two had a terrible resemblance to a child forcing a kitten's nose into a saucer of milk to compel it to drink" (Chapter 21).

Two major points are to be made here, in addition to marking the clearly erotic nature of the descriptions. These are, in the main, the major sexual scenes and descriptions in the novel; they are not only undeniably sexual,[34] but also incestuous, especially when taken together, as we shall see.

To consider the first point, only relations with vampires are sexualized in this novel; indeed, a deliberate attempt is made to make sexuality seem unthinkable in "normal relations" between the sexes. All the close relationships, including those between Lucy and her three suitors and Mina and her husband, are spiritualized beyond credibility. Only when Lucy becomes a vampire is she allowed to be "voluptuous," yet she must have been so long before, judging from her effect on men and from Mina's description of her. (Mina, herself, never physically described, never suffers the fate of voluptuousness before or after being bitten, for reasons which will become apparent.) Thus, vampirism is associated not only with death, immortality, and orality, but also with sexuality.

Further, in psychoanalytic terms, the vampirism is a manifestation of greatly desired and equally strongly feared fantasies. These fantasies have encouraged critics to point to the Oedipus complex at the center of the novel. Dracula, for example, is seen as the "father-figure of huge potency,"[35] and he "even aspires to be, in a sense, the father of the band that is pursuing him. Because he intends, as he tells them, to turn them all into vampires, he will be their creator and therefore 'father.' "[36] The major focus of the novel, then, would appear to be the battle of the sons against the father to release the desired woman, the mother, she whom it is felt originally belonged to the son till the father seduced her away: "the set-up reminds one rather of the primal horde as pictured somewhat fantastically perhaps by Freud in *Totem and Taboo*, with the brothers banding together against the father who has tried to keep all the females to himself."[37]

Moreover, the Oedipal rivalry is not merely a matter of the Van Helsing group, in which "Van Helsing represents the good father figure,"[38] pitted against the Big Daddy, Dracula. Rather, from the novel's beginning, a marked rivalry among the men is evident, one with which we are familiar from almost all of Stoker's fiction. This rivalry is defended against by the constant, almost obsessive, assertion of the value of friendship and *agape* among members of the Van Helsing group. Specifically, the defense of overcompensation is employed, most often by Van Helsing in his assertions of esteem for Dr. Seward and his friends. The others, too, repeat expressions of mutual affection *ad nauseum*: they clearly protest too much. Perhaps this is most obviously symbolized, and unintentionally exposed, by the blood transfusions from Arthur, Seward, Quincey Morris, and Van Helsing to Lucy Westenra. The great friendship among rivals for Lucy's hand lacks credibility and is especially strained when Van Helsing makes it clear that the transfusions (merely the reverse of the vampire's bloodletting) are in their nature sexual; Van Helsing's warning to Seward not to tell Arthur that anyone else has given Lucy blood indicates the sexual nature of the operation.[39] Furthermore, Arthur himself feels that, as a result of having given Lucy his blood, they are in effect married. Thus, the friendships of the novel mask a deep-seated rivalry and hostility.

*Dracula* does then appear to enact the Oedipal rivalry among sons and between the son and the father for the affections of the mother. The fantasy of patricide and its acting out is obviously satisfying. According to Norman Holland, such a threatening wish-fulfillment can be rewarding only when properly defended against or associated with other pleasurable fantasies. Among the other fantasies are those of life after death, the triumph of "good over evil," mere man over superhuman forces, and the rational West over the mysterious East.[40] Most likely not frightening and certainly intellectualized, these simplistic abstractions provide a diversion from more threatening material and assure the fantast that God's in his heaven, all's right with the world. On the surface, this is the moral of the end of the novel: Dracula is safely reduced to ashes, Mina is cleansed, the "boys" are triumphant. Seemingly, then, the reader of *Dracula* identifies with those who are doing battle against the evil in this world, against Count Dracula. On the surface of it, this is where one's sympathies lie in reading the novel.

However, what is far more significant in the interrelation of fantasy and defense is the duplication of characters and structure which betrays an identification with Dracula and a fantasy of matricide underlying the more obvious patricidal wishes, a fantasy for which we have been prepared by our analysis of Stoker's other novels.

As observed, the split between the sexual vampire family and the asexual Van Helsing group is not at all clear-cut: Jonathan, Van Helsing, Seward and Holmwood are all overwhelmingly attracted to the vampires, to sexuality. Fearing this, they employ two defenses, projection and denial: it is not we who want the vampires, it is they who want us (to eat us, to seduce us, to kill us). Despite the projections, we should recall that almost all the onstage killing is done by the "good guys": that of Lucy, of the vampire women, and of Dracula. The projection of the wish to kill onto the vampires wears thinnest perhaps when Dr. Seward, contemplating the condition of Lucy, asserts that "had she then to be killed I could have done it with savage delight" (Chapter 16). Even earlier, when Dr. Seward is rejected by Lucy, he longs for a cause with which to distract himself from the pain of rejection: "Oh, Lucy, Lucy, I cannot be angry with you. . . . If I only could have as strong a cause as my poor mad friend there [significantly, he refers to Renfield]—a good, unselfish cause to make me work—that would be indeed happiness" (Chapter 11). Seward's wish is immediately fulfilled by Lucy's vampirism and the subsequent need to destroy her.

Obviously, the acting out of such murderous impulses is threatening: in addition to the defenses mentioned above, the use of religion not only to exorcise the evil but to justify the murders is striking. In other words, Christianity is on our side, we *must* be right. In this connection, it is helpful to mention the name "Lord Godalming" (the point is repeated).[41] Additional justification is provided by the murdered themselves: the peace into which they subside is to be read as a thank you note. Correlated with the religious defense is one described by Freud in *Totem and Taboo* in which the violator of the taboo can avert disaster by Lady MacBeth-like compulsive rituals and renunciations.[42] The repeated use of the Host, the complicated ritual of the slaying of the vampires, and the ostensible, though not necessarily conscious, renunciation of sexuality are the penance paid by those in *Dracula* who violate the taboos against incest and the murder of parents.

Since we now see that Dracula acts out the repressed fantasies of the other male characters, since those others wish to do what he can do, we have no difficulty in recognizing an identification with the aggressor on the part of characters and reader alike. Indeed, this identification between male characters and Dracula is physically manifest in the complementary doubling between the Dracula we meet early in the novel and the deteriorating Harker. Indeed, we recall the horror with which Harker observes Dracula returning from the kill dressed in his—Harker's—clothing, "as if it had been given him to encounter an aspect of himself in Transylvania with which he was doomed to merge. In the course of the novel he and Dracula, pivoting around Mina, whom they both love, slowly change place and form. It is a strange transformation in which via Mina, Harker has been weakened by a succubus, who in turn nourishes her incubus, the ever more youthful Dracula. It will be seen too, that except for the final moments of the fiction, Harker becomes increasingly more supine as Dracula grows more active."[43] It is important, then, to see what it is that Dracula is after.

The novel tells of two major episodes, the seductions of Lucy and Mina, to which the experience of Harker at Castle Dracula provides a prologue and a hero, one whose narrative encloses the others and with whom, therefore, one might readily identify. This, however, is both a defense against and a disguise for the central identification of the novel with Dracula and his sexual assaults on the women. It is relevant in this context to observe how spontaneous and ultimately trivial Dracula's interest in Harker is. When Harker arrives at Castle Dracula, his host makes a lunge for him, but only after Harker has cut his finger and is bleeding. Dracula manages to control himself and we hear no more about his interest in Harker's blood until the scene with the vampire women when he says, "This man belongs to me!" (Chapter 3) and, again a little later, "have patience. Tonight is mine. To-morrow night is yours!" (Chapter 4). After this we hear no more of Dracula's interest in Jonathan; indeed, when Dracula arrives in England, he never again goes after Jonathan. For his part, Jonathan appears far more concerned about the vampire women than about Dracula—they are more horrible and fascinating to him. Indeed, Harker is relieved to be saved from the women by Dracula. Moreover, the novel focuses far more extensively on the Lucy and Mina episodes from which, at first, the Jonathan episodes may seem disconnected; actually, they are not, but we can only see why after we understand what is going on in the rest of the novel.

In accepting the notion of identification with the aggressor in *Dracula*, what we accept is an understanding of the reader's identification with the aggressor's victimization of women. Dracula both desires Lucy and Mina and wills their destruction. What this means is obvious when we recall that his attacks on these two closest of friends seem incredibly coincidental on the narrative level. Only on a deeper level is there no coincidence at all: the level on which one recognizes that Lucy and Mina are essentially

the same figure.[44] Moreover, the ambivalence becomes understand-
able once we recognize that this figure is the mother, an identification explicit in the text. In the initial and aborted seduction of
Harker by the vampire women, Stoker reveals both Jonathan's
ambivalence and the identity of the women. Interestingly, Harker
seeks out this episode by violating the count's (father's) injunc-
tion to remain in his room: "let me warn you with all seriousness,
that should you leave these rooms you will not by any chance
go to sleep in any other part of the castle." This, of course, is
what Harker promptly does. When Dracula breaks in and discovers
Harker with the vampire women, he acts like a jealous husband
and an irate father as well: "His eyes were positively blazing. The
red light in them was lurid. . . . 'How dare you touch him, any
of you?' " (Chapter 3). Jonathan's role as child here is reinforced
by the fact that, when Dracula takes him away from the women,
he gives them a child as substitute.

But most instructive is Jonathan's perspective as he awaits, in
a state of erotic arousal, the embraces of the vampire women,
especially the fair one: "The other was fair as fair can be, with
great wavy masses of golden hair and eyes like pale sapphires. I
seemed somehow to know her face and to know it in connection
with some dreamy fear, but I could not recollect at the moment
now or where" (Chapter 3). As far as we know, Jonathan never
recollects, but we should be able to understand that the face is
that of the mother (almost archetypally presented), she whom
he desires yet fears, the temptress-seductress, Medusa. Moreover,
this golden girl reappears in the early description of Lucy who,
as "bloofer lady," preys on children. Lucy is as attractive and
threatening to the children as the vampire women are to Jonathan.

In its depiction of women *Dracula* employs the conventional
fair/dark opposition, Lucy, for example, being transformed from
a fair and lovely maiden to a sinister and darkly voluptuous vampire (thus reinforcing the understanding of the fair female at
the castle as mother, albeit mother as vampire): early in the story,
when Lucy is not completely vampirized, Dr. Seward describes
her hair "in its usual sunny ripples" (Chapter 12); later, when

the men watch her return to her tomb, Lucy is described as "a dark-haired woman" (Chapter 16).[45] While Mina's coloring is never specified, for which there is good reason as we shall see, once assaulted by Dracula, Mina is stained with the mark of Cain.

The dark stain of the vampire woman, equivalent to the portrayal of fallen women in eighteenth- and nineteenth-century fiction, is associated with sexual aggressiveness.[46] Indeed, the argument has been advanced that the vampire women are examples of sex-role reversal, with the women assuming the active, aggressive role, allowing the males to enjoy a passive sexual position. We should recall especially Harker's catalepticlike stupor when approached by the vampire sisters or while Mina sucks at Dracula's breast. Clearly, Stoker is both employing and reversing a number of conventional stereotypes: "vampire women not only reject motherhood, they dine on children, as special gourmet items peculiar to the female palates. . . ."[47] Moreover, the portrayal of Mina as an extraordinary woman with the mind of a man, one who provides maternal nurturance for all of the male characters, as well as the means to destroy Dracula—both through her transcriptions of journal and phonograph accounts and through her telepathic rapport with the count—anticipates Stoker's later depictions of the strong, intelligent, and independent Marjory Drake and Stephen Norman, of *The Mystery of the Sea* and *The Man*, respectively.

However, the facile and stereotypical dichotomy between the dark woman and the fair, the fallen and the idealized, the sexualized and the saintly is sustained on the surface throughout *Dracula*. Indeed, among the more gratuitous passages in the novel are those in which the "New Woman" who is sexually aggressive is verbally assaulted. Mina Harker remarks that such a woman, whom she holds in contempt, "will do the proposing herself" (Chapter 8). Additionally, we must compare Van Helsing's hope "that there are good women still left to make life happy" (Chapter 14) with Mina's assertion that "the world seems full of good men— even if there *are* monsters in it" (Chapter 17). A remarkable contrast! Perhaps nowhere is the dichotomy of sensual and sexless women more dramatic than it is in *Dracula*, and nowhere is the suddenly sexual woman more violently and self-righteously persecuted than in Stoker's thriller.

Divided into three major sections, *Dracula* begins with the Harker prologue portraying the exciting and threatening seduction by the mother. The rest of the novel comprises a revenge story of matricide told twice. In the first telling, the mother is more desirable, more sexual, more threatening, and must be destroyed. In Lucy's depiction we see concrete evidence that "the vampires . . . suggest not marauding sexual assault so much as awakening sexuality." However, the sexuality, once awakened, is terrifying, requiring for its defeat "all the resources of society and religion.[48] Not only is Lucy the more sexualized figure, she is the more rejecting figure, rejecting two of the three "sons" in the novel. This section of the book ends with her destruction, not by Dracula but by the man whom she was to marry. The novel could not end here, though; the story had to be told again to assuage the anxiety occasioned by matricide. In the second telling, the mother is much less sexually threatening and is ultimately rescued, as are numerous Stoker heroines. In *Dracula*, certainly, and to some extent in all Stoker's horror tales, the rescue motif is linked to this splitting of the female image into the configuration Freud describes as mother/prostitute.[49] Stoker, of course, is by no means alone in this depiction of female characters. Nonetheless, in *Dracula*, the split between the sexualized female and the madonna is especially vivid and obvious. The consequence of this perception of women is both the ambivalence toward and the doubling of Lucy and Mina we have described.

Perhaps the story needed to be retold because the desire to destroy the mother was originally too close to the surface to be satisfying; certainly, the reader would not be comfortable had the novel ended with Arthur's murder of Lucy. The desire to destroy Mina is more skillfully disguised, more successfully defended against, both for the reader and for the characters.[50] Moreover, Mina is never described physically and is the opposite of rejecting: all of the men become her sons, symbolized by the naming of her actual son after them all.

Mina indeed acts and is treated as both the saint and the mother (ironically, this is particularly clear when she comforts Arthur for the loss of Lucy). She is all good, all pure.[51] When, however, she is seduced away from the straight and narrow by Dracula, she is "unclean," tainted, and stained with a mark on her forehead immediately occasioned by Van Helsing's touching her forehead with the Host. Van Helsing's hostility toward Mina is further revealed when he cruelly reminds her of her "intercourse" with Dracula: " 'Do you forget,' he said, with actually a smile, 'that last night he banqueted heavily and will sleep late?' " (Chapter 22). The hostility is so obvious that the other men are shocked.[52]

Nevertheless, the "sons," and the reader as well, identify with Dracula's attack on Mina; indeed, the men cause it, as indicated by the events which transpire when all the characters are at Seward's hospital-asylum.[53] The members of the brotherhood go out at night to seek out Dracula's lairs, and they leave Mina undefended at the hospital. They claim that this insures her safety; in fact, it insures the reverse: the real purpose in leaving Mina out of the plans and in the hospital is to insure her vulnerability. They have clear indications in Renfield's warning of what is to happen to her, and they all, especially her husband, observe that she is not well and seems to be getting weaker. That they could rationalize these signs away while looking for and finding them everywhere else further indicates that they are avoiding seeing what they want to ignore; in other words, they want Dracula to get her. This is not to deny that they also want to save Mina; it is simply to claim that the ambivalence toward the mother is fully realized in the novel.

At the end of his prologue, Jonathan exclaims, "I am alone in the castle with those awful women. Faugh! Mina is a woman, and there is nought in common." Clearly, there is. Mina at the breast of Count Dracula is identical to the vampire women whose desire is to draw out of the male the fluid necessary for life.

That this is viewed as an act of castration is evident from Jonathan's conclusion: "At least God's mercy is better than that of these monsters, and the precipice is steep and high. At its foot a man may sleep—*as a man*. Good-bye, all! Mina!" (Chapter 4; my italics).

We can now return to that ambivalence and, I believe, with the understanding of the significance and power of the mother figure, comprehend the precise perspective of the novel. Several critics have correctly emphasized the regression to both orality and anality in *Dracula*.[54] Certainly, the sexuality is perceived in oral terms. The primal scene already mentioned makes abundantly clear that intercourse is perceived in terms of nursing: "Stoker is describing a symbolic act of enforced fellatio, where blood is again a substitute for semen, and where a chaste female suffers a violation that is essentially sexual. Of particular interest in the passage is the striking image of 'a child forcing a kitten's nose into a saucer of milk to compel it to drink,' suggesting an element of regressive infantilism in the vampire superstition."[55] The scene referred to is, in several senses, the climax of the novel; it is the most explicit view of the act of vampirism and is, therefore, all the more significant as an expression of the nature of sexual intercourse as the novel depicts it. Moreover, the description affirms the identification of sexuality with destruction. In it, the woman is doing the sucking.

While it is true that the reader may most often think of Dracula as the active partner,[56] and certainly many of the plays and films so present him, the scenes of detailed and explicit sexuality are described from the male perspective, with the females as the active assailants.[57] And, in this climactic scene, the role of Dracula is complex and revealing. More obviously threatening to Mina than ever before, Dracula is viewed here as the mother suckling her child. Thus, again, it is the female who is most actively threatening. Only the acts of phallic aggression,[58] the killings of all the vampires including Lucy, involve the males in active roles. *Dracula*, then, dramatizes the child's view of intercourse as a wounding and a killing. But the primary preoccupation, as attested to by the behavior of both Mina and Dracula in the primal scene, is with the role of the female in the act. Thus, it is not surprising that the central anxiety of the novel is the fear of the devouring woman.[59]

The threatening pre-Oedipal fantasy, the regression to a primary oral obsession, the attraction and destruction of the vampires of *Dracula* are, then, interrelated and interdependent. What they spell out is a fusion of the memory of nursing at the mother's breast with a primal scene fantasy which produces the fear that the sexually desirable woman will annihilate if she is not first destroyed. The fantasy of incest and matricide evokes the mythic image of the *vagina dentata* evident in so many folk tales[60] in which the mouth and the vagina are identified with one another by the primitive mind and pose the threat of castration to all men until the teeth are extracted by the hero. The conclusion of *Dracula*, the "salvation" of Mina, is equivalent to such an "extraction": Mina will not remain the *vagina dentata* to threaten them all.

Central to the structure and unconscious theme of *Dracula* is, then, primarily the desire to destroy the threatening mother, she who threatens by being desirable. Otto Rank best explains why it is Dracula whom the novel seems to portray as the threat when he says, in a study which is pertinent to ours: "through the displacement of anxiety on to the father, the renunciation of the mother, necessary for the sake of life is assured. For this feared father prevents the return to the mother and thereby the releasing of the much more painful primary anxiety, which is related to the mother's genitals as the place of birth and later transferred to objects taking the place of the genitals [such as the mouth]."[61] Finally, the novel has it both ways: Dracula is destroyed[62] and Van Helsing saved; Lucy is destroyed and Mina saved. The novel ends on a rather ironic note, given our understanding here, as Harker concludes with a quote from the good father, Van Helsing: "We want no proofs; we ask none to believe us! This boy will some day know what a brave and gallant woman his mother is. Already he knows her sweetness and loving care; later on he will understand how some men so loved her, that they did dare so much for her sake" (Chapter 27).

As the preceding analyses of *Dracula* and of Stoker's fiction in general indicate, *Dracula* is the most complex, fully worked out, and compelling of Stoker's stories, one which nonetheless reveals all of Stoker's major themes and fantasies, strengths and weaknesses as a writer. In its painstaking sustaining of suspense, its evocation of horror, its visions of nightmare landscapes, it is Stoker at his very finest; and in its questioning of the boundaries between life and death, the real and the fantastic, and its ambivalent portrayal of women and of men's response to women, it is Stoker at his most interesting.

Clearly in the Gothic tradition, *Dracula* is replete with characters who superficially resemble those of sentimental fiction and who are ostensibly engaged in conflict between the opposed forces of a facilely conceived right and wrong. However, as a late manifestation of the Gothic, *Dracula* reveals, upon closer scrutiny, a far more complex rendering of the nature of evil and the threat of sexuality than its early predecessors. The appeal of *Dracula* derives, not only from its masterful sustaining of suspense and its nightmarish depiction of landscape, castle, and cemetery, but from its portrait of a seemingly universal horror—the horror of the human mind faced with its own desires for sexual fusion and violence.

We have made little mention so far of the appeal of the "undead," the seduction of immortality which is so manifestly a component of Dracula's portrait, and one which others have remarked. In the present analysis, this theme does not exist apart from Stoker's depiction of women, specifically as mother. We should recall the questioning of female nature in *The Man*, the archetypal mother of "The Shadow Builder," the nature of Lady Arabella in *The Lair of the White Worm*, the ambiguous vitality of Queen Tera in *The Jewel of Seven Stars* and of the Voivoda Teuta and Rupert's mother in *The Lady of the Shroud*. In all of these instances, the female characters are ambivalently portrayed. Often seemingly both living and dead or chaste and promiscuous, spiritual and animal, woman in Stoker's fiction achieves fullest realization in Lucy and Mina, woman as both mother and vampire, source of life, death and life eternal.

While the Gothic tradition in general is distinguished by its portrayal of "the attractive fascination of the monster . . . , in *Dracula* the fear of and fascination with women is a pulsating theme of the fiction. In *The Lair of the White Worm* the fear and fascination are writhing, horrid presences. Both books, earnestly examined, make one wonder just how genial Bram Stoker's inner life could have been."[63] Moreover, when we recall that, as a child, Stoker remained bedridden till the age of seven, with the expectation that he might never live to arise from the supine, and that during these years he was nursed by a strong woman who nourished both his life and his invalidism while she told him horror tales of plagues and banshees, worked, and gave birth to four more children, we can begin to gain a sense of possible biographical sources of his ambivalent obsession with women.

Finally, *Dracula* succeeds because it realizes a perfect balance between terrifying but desired fantasies and appropriate defenses which were certainly workable in Victorian England with its notorious splitting of rational West and mysterious East, mother and whore, right and wrong, and its repression of sexuality, defenses which have not lost their viability today. What Stoker provides in *Dracula* is the means for us to enact our fascination and attraction, our repulsion and violent impulses while remaining at least partially unaware of our more threatening desires, those both loving and murderous. As Philip Hallie puts it in his essay on horror and cruelty, the reader "too feels this awe before an immense power, he too 'identifies' with both the suffering victim and the acting villain. Like the horror of the victim, his horror is a commingling of desire and disgust, of admiration and the desire to participate in immense power, as well as fear for his own life."[64]

In choosing the vampire as the particular manifestation for his combination of the Wandering Jew/Byronic hero/overreacher, Stoker was working in a tradition which included, among the romantics, the works not only of Mary Shelley, but of Byron (see "Manfred," "Cain," and "The Giaour"), Keats ("La Belle Dame sans Merci" and "Lamia"), Coleridge ("Christabel" and "The Rime of the Ancient Mariner"), and Goethe, to name but a few,[65] as well as considering subjects similar to those of such contemporaneous works as "Heart of Darkness," and anticipating some of the works of Franz Kafka, for example.

As is true elsewhere in the tradition, the dark spirit in *Dracula* is proud and haughty, tortured and desperate. Mina makes quite explicit that we are to experience pity as well as horror in contemplation of the count, saying "That poor soul who has wrought all this misery is the saddest case of all. Just think what will be his joy when he, too, is destroyed in his worser part that his better part may have spiritual immortality. You must be pitiful to him, too . . ." (Chapter 23). Moreover, since Mina is explicitly comparing both herself and Lucy to Dracula in this passage, the reflection of the human in the vampire is quite apparent, engaging our sympathies with villain as well as hero, two halves of the one self.

As we have seen so far with particular emphasis on the female characters in Stoker's fiction, Stoker employed doubling and splitting of characters as a device for realizing human nature in its ambiguity. More than a fictional device, this technique reflects a psychological reality for Stoker, one on which many of his interests and occupations were based. Leonard Wolf remarks that "the most enigmatic relationship of Stoker's life is . . . the one he had with the actor Henry Irving. . . ."[66] In our final chapter, we will recall this relationship in the context of Stoker's interest in the doubling of identities.

## Chapter Six
# Conclusion: Fictional Doubles and Famous Imposters

In concluding our study of the life and work of Bram Stoker, we can focus directly on the recurrent theme in Stoker's writing of perceived dualities in human existence, often represented in the merging or doubling of identities. In the fiction, typically subordinate to the ambivalent portrayals of the female characters, duplications or splittings of identity are more a technique for creating character complexity than a theme directly explored. In *The Man*, for instance, Stephen Norman is initially described as both masculine and feminine; her task is to resolve her confusion and her destiny is to become a "true woman"—despite her name. In the novels in which characters constitute an Oedipal configuration, Stoker employs two rather conventional types of doubling of characters to define the conflict. Typically, the female characters are doubled by splitting into, in the extreme cases, the opposites of Madonna and whore. This is most clearly evident in *Dracula*, of course, but we have seen paler versions of the splitting in *The Jewel of Seven Stars* and *The Lady of the Shroud*. In Stoker's weakest novels, *Miss Betty* and *The Lair of the White Worm*, the female characters are either all good or all evil, respectively, and, consequently, less complex and less credible.

The doubling of male characters in the novels, except in the case of *Dracula*, is limited to doubling by addition: that is, several virtuous heroes are banded together (despite evident sibling rivalry) to save the heroine. In *Dracula*, to the extent to which the count doubles with members of the Van Helsing group—specifically, Jonathan Harker and Van Helsing himself, the only

two men tempted by the vampire women at Castle Dracula—
the doubling reflects a splitting similar to that employed in Stoker's
portrayal of the female characters: the heroes themselves are
dual in nature and desire. The doubling of characters is, then,
the means most often employed by Stoker to portray character
complexity and conflict.

Moreover, the characteristic poles of the doubling reflect a
recurrent concern about the antitheses good-evil, spiritual-animal,
and their conflict within the human soul. As we have seen, throughout Stoker's fiction, the best in the human spirit always triumphs
over an evil which is typically, if only symbolically, depicted as
sexual. Thus, at the end of his preternatural Pilgrim's Progress,
the rational Christian hero exorcises vampires, a centuries' old
white worm, and an Egyptian queen, destroying lustful Turkish
heathens, malevolent usurers and Spaniards, and dissolute hypno-
tists, while reclaiming the truly penitent. As reward, this Victorian
St. George—or St. Patrick—receives treasures and the hand of a
purified maiden whose love is all that the good mother should
provide.

This allegorical level of significance in Stoker's fiction corre-
sponds to some of the great debates and concerns of the Victorian
era which arose from the clash of Darwinian materialism with the
views of organized religion. In *Dracula*, Stoker comes closest to
a direct consideration of the opposition between those who believe in the irreducibility of the human spirit and those who would
reduce all to mere palpitating protoplasm, embodying the extremes
in the heterodox Abraham Van Helsing and the supermaterialist
Count Dracula.[1]

Stoker's dualistic conception of human nature, then, was both
historically and literarily influenced, and his consequent employment of character doubling, a natural choice. Not only is the
Gothic tradition rife with doppelgänger tales and motifs, but
Stoker himself was apparently psychologically disposed to a
fascination with boundaries, boundaries between one identity and
another and boundaries between male and female, life and death,
spirit and flesh.

### Famous Imposters

*Famous Imposters* (1910), Stoker's third nonfiction book (counting *The Duties of the Clerks of the Petty Sessions*, 1879), deals directly and rather differently with the phenomenon of doublings: here, Stoker directs his attention to impostures and frauds. Rather than reflecting a mystical apprehension of human dualities, *Famous Imposters* is deliberately concerned with exposing duplicities, debunking pretensions, and demystifying deceptions and hoaxes. The very first sentence of the book makes this goal clear: "The subject of imposture is always an interesting one, and impostors in one shape or another are likely to flourish as long as human nature remains what it is, and society shows itself ready to be gulled."[2] Clearly, for Stoker, one boundary should not be violated, that between fiction and fact, the theater and the throne: what is a subject of fascination and a technique of symbolism in the fiction is often the object of contempt in real life operations.

Divided into ten sections, *Famous Imposters* is written by one "whose largest experiences [have] lain in the field of fiction, [and who] has aimed at dealing with his material as with the material for a novel, except that all the facts given are real and authentic" (*F*, v). The materials and subjects for the study were probably both accumulated and researched throughout the years, in the British Museum and over midnight suppers in the Beefsteak Room at the Lyceum. Anecdotal in format, most of the accounts systematically detail the historical and familial events precipitating and facilitating the imposture, clarifying the nature and extent both of the deceptions and of human gullibility. The book is divided into the following sections: (1) Pretenders (to royalty); (2) Practitioners of Magic; (3) The Wandering Jew; (4) John Law; (5) Witchcraft and Clairvoyance; (6) Arthur Orton (Tichborne claimant); (7) Women as Men; (8) Hoaxes, etc.; (9) Chevalier d'Eon; (10) The Bisley Boy.

In addition to considering mythical or historical figures mentioned or alluded to in the fiction (for example, the discussions of the Wandering Jew or of Mesmer under "Practitioners of Magic"), the book is noteworthy for the exceptions to its self-assigned task of demystification. Most of the exceptions concern women as impostors, and reflect Stoker's mingled conservative and liberationist impulses: they include cases in which the imposture has been imposed upon unwilling victims, such as those accused of being witches in the sixteenth and seventeenth centuries; or cases in which women posed as men in order to function in roles both honorable and yet denied to them by society. We can perhaps hear Charlotte Stoker's accents in her son's statement that "It is not to be wondered at that such attempts are made; or that they were made more often formerly when social advancement had not enlarged the scope of work available for women. The legal and economic disabilities of the gentler sex stood then so fixedly in the way of working opportunity that women desirous of making an honest livelihood took desperate chances to achieve their object" (F, 227).

The most interesting of the impostures discussed in the book, especially so because it claims more of Stoker's time and credulousness than any other, is that of the "Bisley Boy" or the real identity of Queen Elizabeth I. While Stoker stops short of arguing that Elizabeth was indeed a man, he does suggest that the surmise is not only possible, but probable. Conducting his research and argument like the lawyer he studied to be, and aware that the analysis is both a new one (he seems to suggest it is he who is introducing it to the public) and speculative, he warns his reader that "almost from the very start of earnest inquiry it became manifest that here was a subject which could not be altogether put aside or made light of" (F, vii). And, indeed, he does not, spending a great deal of time and effort following up rumors, genealogies, historical personae, matching dates, physiologies, and personalities. It is this final chapter in *Famous Imposters* which most clearly connects Stoker's concerns and skills as a researcher with those already described for the fiction, demonstrating the moves from questioning, to imagining possibilities, to discerning probabilities, to creating imaginative realities, most successfully achieved in *Dracula*.

Interesting on its own account, *Famous Imposters* clarifies Stoker's concern about boundaries, for while he is angrily determined to expose the duplicitous and fraudulent, defined in particular as those who travesty and exploit both human eagerness to believe and genuine spirituality, and to ascertain what is empirically demonstrable, he is no materialist. *Famous Imposters* is, then, another demonstration of Stoker's lifelong dualism: his belief in the mysterious dimensions of persons and events and in the dichotomy between the empirical and the spiritual. Often witty and vivid, *Famous Imposters* reinforces the perspective of Stoker as one comfortable in both of his worlds: the practical and mundane on the one hand, the imaginative and often bizarre on the other. For Stoker as author and acting manager for Henry Irving, all of life was full of dramatic possibilities, one of which he embodied so vividly as to give a particular and irrevocable shape to certain of our most harrowing and recurrent of nightmares.

## Bram Stoker and Henry Irving

In concluding with the most important relationship of Stoker's adult life, that with Henry Irving, we can discern ways in which the themes of the fictions were continuous with those of the life and, therefore, we can begin to understand the life as a whole, the figure under the carpet, in Leon Edel's rephrasing of Henry James's famous image.

Early in the *Personal Reminiscences of Henry Irving*, Stoker recounts the episode which marked the beginning of what can only be termed his union with Henry Irving. It was only his second meeting with the great actor, but it followed upon and occurred in response to Stoker's laudatory reviews of Irving's performances published in the *Dublin Mail*. With several others, Stoker was invited by Irving to a dinner after which, Stoker tells us, Irving announced that he would recite for Stoker the narrative poem "The Dream of Eugene Aram" by Thomas Hood.

As a poem, "The Dream of Eugene Aram" is not especially distinguished; as a vehicle for what Stoker took to be a transcendently artful performance and as a reflection of themes resonating in Stoker's fiction, it is significant. In his description of the event, Stoker wishes to leave no doubt regarding Irving's talent or his own susceptibilities. Listing other dramatic speeches he had heard, Stoker describes Irving's performance as follows:

. . . such was Irving's commanding force, so great was the magnetism of his genius, so profound was the sense of his dominance that I sat spellbound. Outwardly I was of stone; nought quick in me but receptivity and imagination. That I knew the story and was even familiar with its unalterable words was nothing. The whole thing was new, recreated by a force of passion which was like a new power. . . . here was incarnate power, incarnate passion, so close to one that one could meet it eye to eye, within touch of one's outstretched hand. The surroundings became non-existent; the dress ceased to be noticeable; recurring thoughts of self-existence were not at all. Here was indeed Eugene Aram as he was face to face with his Lord; his very soul aflame in the light of his abiding horror. Looking back now I can realise the perfection of art with which the mind was led and swept and swayed, hither and thither as the actor wished. How a change of tone or time denoted the personality of the "Blood-avenging Sprite" —and how the nervous, eloquent hands slowly moving, outspread fanlike, round the fixed face—set as doom, with eyes as inflexible as Fate—emphasised it till one instinctively quivered with pity. Then the awful horror on the murderer's face as the ghost in his brain seemed to take external shape before his eyes, and enforced on him that from his sin there was no refuge. After the climax of horror the Actor was able by art and habit to control himself to the narrative mood whilst he spoke the few concluding lines of the poem.
Then he collapsed half fainting. . . .
As to its effect I had no adequate words. I can only say that after a few seconds of stony silence following his collapse I burst into something like hysterics. (PR, 1:29–31)

Following this admission, Stoker feels the need to qualify his reaction with one of the longest autobiographical statements in the

*Personal Reminiscences,* a statement in which he describes both his early invalidism and his great psychological and physical strength as an adult.

His conclusion to the episode is also worth quoting at length, as much for what is not said as for what is.

> In those moments of our mutual emotion he too had found a friend and knew it. Soul had looked into soul! From that hour began a friendship as profound, as close, as lasting as can be between two men.
>
> He has gone his road. Now he lies amongst the great dead. . . .
>
> And the sight of his picture before me, with those loving words, the record of a time of deep emotion and full understanding of us both, each for the other, unmans me once again as I write. . . .
>
> I have ventured to write fully, if not diffusely, about not only my first meeting with Irving but about matters which preceded it and in some measure lead to an understanding of its results.
>
> When a man with his full share of ambition is willing to yield it up to work with a friend whom he loves and honours, it is perhaps as well that in due season he may set out his reasons for so doing. Such is but just; and I now place it on record for the sake of Irving as well as of myself, and for the friends of us both.
>
> For twenty-seven years I worked with Henry Irving, helping him in all honest ways in which one man may aid another—and there were no ways with Irving other than honourable.
>
> Looking back I cannot honestly find any moment in my life when I failed him, or when I put myself forward in any way when the most scrupulous good taste could have enjoined or even suggested a larger measure of reticence.
>
> By my dealing with him I am quite content to be judged, now and hereafter. . . . (*PR,* 1:33–34)

Clearly, Stoker's response to Irving reflects an experiencing of emotional intensity significant to him, an intensity which fascinated him but which he feared might be misunderstood.

That Stoker was profoundly and essentially moved by Irving's performance is undeniable, and some speculation regarding the convergence of factors causing this emotional upheaval will reward the reader interested in gaining a sense of the unity under-

lying the variety of Stoker's pursuits, a unity best expressed as
that fascination with boundaries we have mentioned. The trans-
gression of boundaries manifested in the Gothic marked a number
of the plays performed by the Irving Company and managed by
Stoker, from *The Flying Dutchman*, an adaptation of which
Stoker and Irving devised early in their collaboration, through the
abortive mounting of *Dante* late in Irving's career. The theme of
boundaries was evidently one which fascinated Irving as well
for, according to Stoker, he and Irving and Hall Caine (the writer
and critic to whom *Dracula* is dedicated) spent hours discussing
the boundaries between mortality and eternal life and the nature
of sin and conflict in the human heart, underlying which is a
passion Stoker sought in all his endeavors. Here is Stoker's description of Irving's *Hamlet*, excerpted from his review:

There is another view of Hamlet, too, which Mr. Irving seems to
realise by a kind of instinct, but which requires to be more fully and
intentionally worked out. . . . The great, deep, underlying idea of Hamlet is that of a mystic. . . . In the high-strung nerves of the man; in the
natural impulse of spiritual susceptibility; in his concentrated action
spasmodic though it sometimes be, and in the divine delirium of his
perfected passion, there is the instinct of the mystic which he has but
to render a little plainer, in order that the less susceptible senses of his
audience may see and understand. (*PR*, 1:26–27)

It is indeed the sensibility and susceptibilities of the mystic in
Stoker to which Irving appealed and which are reflected in
Stoker's fictions as well.

More specifically, the themes of "Eugene Aram" are superbly
calculated, in collusion with Irving's performance, to have transformed Stoker's life. "The Dream of Eugene Aram," a narrative
in verse form, tells the tale of a boys' school usher who, unlike
the "four-and-twenty happy boys" who shout and play in all
their innocent boyhood in the first stanzas, broods in great torment about his dream of murder. The Usher tells his tale to one
unusual young boy who, remaining apart from the games of his
fellows, reads a story called "The Death of Abel."

> And down he sat beside the lad,
>   And talked with him of Cain;
>
> And, long since then, of bloody men,
>   Whose deeds tradition saves;
> Of lonely folk cut off unseen,
>   And hid in sudden graves;
> Of horrid stabs, in groves forlorn,
>   And murders done in caves;
>
> And how the sprites of injured men
>   Shriek upward from the sod.—
> Ay, how the ghostly hand will point
>   To show the burial clod. . . .

To the boy, Aram recounts his dream of a particular murder, the murder of "a feeble man and old" whom Aram kills for his gold. Once murdered, however, the old man refuses to remain buried. And like Lady Macbeth, Aram cannot wash the stain from his hands. Not surprisingly, the dream is no dream at all and the poem concludes with the arrest of Eugene Aram "With gyves upon his wrist."

It should be clear that, despite the disturbingly singsong measure of the verse, the convergence of the poem's themes with Irving's stunning performance could not have been better calculated to affect Stoker as it did. The theme of boundaries—here, between life and death, good and evil, dream and reality, wish and fear—is precisely that of the poem's emotional fulcrum. The playing off of the innocence of youth against the guilt of manhood, the inevitability expressed in the use of the Cain story, the masking of the parricidal fantasy with guilt and self-loathing are familiar to us from *Dracula* and the Gothic tradition in general. Compounded by what Stoker saw as Irving's ability to transform himself, physically as well as emotionally, into the role he was playing, the emotional force of the experience on Stoker was predictable.

We might speculate further that, for Stoker, the characterization of Aram and the lone schoolboy reading "The Death of Abel" represented, respectively, Irving and Stoker himself. Moreover, these identities merge, for the lone schoolboy is Aram, too, in his innocent preparation for the Fall. Indeed, the distinguishing of identities and their subsequent merging is an attribute of the *Personal Reminiscenses* as a whole, for in telling Irving's life, Stoker was telling his own as well—a fact evident in the ambiguity of references in the title: *Personal Reminiscences of Henry Irving* may mean both *by* Henry Irving and *about* Henry Irving.

In choosing to spend the next twenty-seven years of his life devoted to Irving, then, Bram Stoker was electing more than a career; he was choosing an identity for himself distinct from yet continuous with that of one whose art was based on the transforming of identities, one whose daily performances confirmed for Stoker his own questionings of boundaries, questionings prevalent throughout the fiction and most fully and lastingly embodied in Count Dracula, a character, we might suppose, written expressly to be performed by Henry Irving (though Irving never did).

Significantly, women, so central in the fiction, are subordinate, if not absent entirely from considerations of Stoker's work with Irving. We may say, without unwarranted speculation, that Stoker's friendship with Irving was the most important love relationship of his adult life. His description of his reaction to Irving's recitation is that of someone who is falling in love, and Stoker's own words seem calculated both to express that fact and to insure that it not be misunderstood, that it not be taken as anything other than an extraordinarily close friendship. Indeed, we may surmise that, if anything, Stoker is idealizing the situation rather than moderating it, for Stoker's relationship with Irving was apparently not without its tensions and rivalries. Most likely, the *Personal Reminiscences* greatly romanticizes Stoker's life at the Lyceum, Stoker failing to describe the roles of others equally close to Irving: specifically, Louis Frederick Austin, Irving's secretary and, often, his speechwriter; Walter Collinson, Irving's valet and dresser; and Harry Loveday, stage manager at the

Lyceum. Austin, annoyed with the competition for Irving's approbation between himself and Stoker, refers, in a letter to his wife, to "that idiot Stoker,"[3] but Austin himself is clearly jealous and truculent. Nonetheless, it is likely that such rivalries did exist among the men close to Irving—and not at all surprising that Stoker did not report them. Laurence Irving claims also that Stoker misunderstood the relationship between Ellen Terry and Henry Irving, portraying it as one of "brotherly affection" and missing the complexity both of their love and their—apparently unconsummated—sexual relationship.[4]

Stoker's idealizations and simplifications of his relationships with those around him and of their dealings with each other is consistent with attributes of the fiction. Specifically, we see similar idealizations of fraternal and filial relations and the simplification of extraordinarily complex heterosexual relations. Perhaps Stoker longed for what he took to be a simpler age, that depicted in the novel of sentiment or, even earlier, in the prose or metrical romance, an age when, as he put it describing the first performance of Irving's he saw, "the answer to insolence was a sword thrust; when only those dare be insolent who could depend to the last on the heart and brain and arm behind the blade" (*PR*, 1:3–4). Certainly, it is this mold in which *Dracula* and many other of Stoker's stories are consciously cast.

However, the fictions also make it evident that Stoker experienced far greater ambivalence and complexity than the *Personal Reminiscences* reveals. Indeed, in his greatest work at least, the balance between tenderness and aggression, desire and fear, lust and adoration, constitutes the success of Stoker's fantasy. And, in story after story, Stoker reenacts the Oedipal rivalry between the son and the father and among brothers and the marked ambivalence toward the mother figure which undoubtedly characterized his childhood, his working life at the Lyceum, and his adult relationships—and which marks the mode of fiction in which he chose primarily to work. As examples of Victorian fiction, his works embody a number of familiar dichotomies: empiricism and mysticism, spirituality and materialism, skepticism and faith, rationality and the unconscious. Not remarkable for subtlety or complexity of vision or characterization, for philosophical or narrative sophistication, for any social concern at all—unlike the greatest Victorian novels—Stoker's work and life are characterized by both a mystical and sentimental sensibility which nonetheless, when embodied in the Gothic fascination with boundaries and ambivalences, brought forth a fantasy of enduring power.

# Notes and References

## Preface

1. Daniel Farson, *The Man Who Wrote Dracula: A biography of Bram Stoker* (New York, 1976), introduction.

2. Published for the Fireside Press by W. Foulsham, London. Farson uses Ludlam for much of his information. Ludlam, in turn, relies heavily on the *Personal Reminiscences*. Unfortunately for both, Ludlam makes a number of small but annoying errors and frequently misquotes. I have relied on Stoker himself in all cases of question or disagreement.

3. See above.

4. In two volumes (New York, 1906).

5. Ludlam, pp. 150–51.

6. Ibid., p. 151.

7. Edited by Charles Osborne (New York, 1973) and reissued in paperback in 1979.

## Chapter One

1. Robert Gittings, *Thomas Hardy's Later Years* (Boston; Little, Brown, 1978), pp. 126, 158–59.

2. *Personal Reminiscences of Henry Irving*, in 2 vols. (London, 1906), 1:31; hereafter cited in the text as *PR*.

3. Ludlam, p. 12.

4. Ibid., p. 14.

5. Ibid., p. 13.

6. Ibid., p. 19.

7. Gay Wilson Allen, *The Solitary Singer* (New York: Macmillan, 1955), p. 467.

8. Ludlam, p. 24.

9. Ibid., p. 46.

10. Farson, p. 33.

11. Ludlam, p. 48.

12. Farson, p. 40.

13. Ludlam, p. 56.

14. Farson, p. 25.

15. Ibid., pp. 50, 54.

16. Ibid., p. 69.

17. Ibid., p. 73.

18. Ludlam, p. 69.

19. Ibid., p. 76.

20. Ibid., p. 78.

21. In *Dracula*, however, Stoker has Van Helsing give credit to "my friend Arminius, of Buda-Pesth University" for information regarding the Count's genealogy (Chapter 18).

22. "The Genesis and Dating of *Dracula* from Bram Stoker's Working Notes," *Notes & Queries* 24, no. 1 (January–February 1977): 39–41.

23. "Account of the Principalities of Wallachia and Moldavia, etc." (London, 1820).

24. An expanded version was published as *The Land Beyond the Forest* (New York: Harper, 1888).

25. See, for example, *PR*, 1:123.

26. Ludlam, p. 98.

27. Stoker allows himself a modest criticism when describing this action of Irving's, saying "it was an unfortunate thing for his own prosperity that Irving did not adhere to the arrangement [we had] made . . . Before he had consulted with me about it, or even told me of it, he had actually signed a tentative acceptance" (*PR*, 2:331).

28. Ludlam, p. 129.

29. Ludlam, p. 146.

30. Ibid., p. 147.

31. Ibid., p. 148.

32. Farson, pp. 233–34. *"Tabes dorsalis"* is, I am informed by Dr. David Goodman of Albany Medical Center, a form of neurosyphilis. Dr. Goodman suggests that Farson misquotes his own doctor who probably suggested that subterfuge of "*non*-specific disease."

33. Ibid.

34. Leon Edel, "The Age of the Archive," *Monday Evening Papers*, no. 7, (Middletown, Conn.: Wesleyan University, Center for Advanced Studies, 1966), p. 14.

35. Leon Edel, "The Figure Under the Carpet," in *Telling Lives*, ed. Marc Pachter (Washington, D.C.: New Republic Books), p. 24.

*Chapter Two*

1. (London, 1909); hereafter cited in the text as *SP*. According to Harry Ludlam, *The Snake's Pass* "appeared as a serial story in . . . several provincial papers late in 1889" ( Ludlam, p. 77).

2. Ludlam, p. 78.

3. The edition used here is from the New English Library (London, 1974); hereafter cited in the text as *MB*.

4. According to *Collier's Encyclopedia*, Sir Robert Walpole (1675–1745) has been regarded frequently as England's first prime minister. A member of Parliament and eloquent orator, Walpole successively became secretary at war, treasurer of the navy, paymaster general of the forces, chancellor of the exchequer, and first lord of the treasury. However, early in his career he was impeached by the Lord of Commons and imprisoned. Though he was to regain power, in his last years he was attacked by many. *Coller's* summarizes his career in a manner which reinforces Stoker's portrait: "By ruthless political methods and a cynical manipulation of men, he achieved the destruction of the Tory Party, security for the Hanoverian dynasty, a stable government with financial strength and administrative efficiency unrivaled in the Europe of his day" (23:226).

5. (London, 1905); hereafter cited in the text as *M*. This edition of *The Man*, the only one I could locate, has no page numbers and seems to be not a final printing, but rather a bound edition of galleys, complete with printer's numbers and replete with errors.

6. See *The Raw & the Cooked: An Introduction to a Science of Mythology*, trans, John and Doreen Weightman (New York: Harper & Row, 1969).

*Chapter Three*

1. Though the text was out of print for many years, it is now available again in two editions. The original was entitled *Under the Sunset*, with illustrations by W. Fitzgerald and W. V. Cockburn (London, 1882). The text has been reprinted by Forgotten Fantasy Library, vol. 17 (1978). Additionally, one can consult Douglas Oliver Street, "Bram Stoker's *Under the Sunset*: An Edition with Introductory Bio-

graphical and Critical Material" (Ph.D. diss., University of Nebraska, 1977); this edition is used here and is cited in the text as *S*.

2. Street, p. v.

3. Ibid., p. vii.

4. See Ludlam, chapter 4, from whom Street also quotes, p. xxxiv.

5. Street (p. cv) sees the influence of Walt Whitman in these passages.

6. *The Gothic Tradition in Fiction* (New York, 1979).

7. Street (pp. xcix–ciii) analyses the influence of Browning and Tennyson evident in this tale.

8. *American Imago* 29 (Summer 1972): 186–98. While Bierman's correlations are perhaps too rigid, almost allegorical themselves, his analyses do highlight the recurrent images and motifs in Stoker's work that we have isolated as well.

9. Bierman makes several correlations here. In addition to the madness, the motifs of eating and sleeping, and the theme of medical detection also in *Dracula*, he sees a correlation to Stoker's life. It is possible, he speculates, that

> The swelling and shrinking in size of the raven, the stress on kith and kin, and on the horoscope suggest very strongly that the powers of seven represent the birth order of the seven Stoker children. After the third power the raven swells, and then starts to shrink to his natural size after the fourth seven is dropped. In oral terms this sequence suggests his mother's pregnancy with the fourth born Tommy who was delivered when Stoker, the third born, was twenty-one months old. The mathematical error by a man who had received honors in mathematics at Trinity College implies not only that he felt Tommy was a mistake, who should have been "wrong multiplied" as No. 7 was, but also that Tommy, number four, should not have been the product of the multiplying, i.e., should not have been born. . . . In fact, when we look at the original sum that causes Tineboy to wish that number seven had never been invented, we find that it is seven to the seventh power which would represent George, the youngest brother, who was born when Stoker was seven. Stoker must have wished, as Mr. Daw did, that George would croak, a word which in Victorian England, also, meant 'die.' This wish is carried out by eating and swallowing and is undone by regurgitation. The

death wishes toward his baby brothers, Tom and George, may be found in *Dracula* in the form of three instances of infanticide by eating and sucking and the frequent usage of the names Tom and George for different minor characters and events. (pp. 192–193)

As we have already seen in the romances, Stoker repeatedly portrays characters who are both part of an Oedipal configuration and presented in rivalry with father or brother figures. It is certainly possible, then, to find further though not conclusive evidence for Bierman's more modest speculations. Indeed, the preoccupations with orality, their correlation with sleeping, eating, and destroying are most fully apparent in *Dracula*, as Bierman claims, and we shall examine Bierman's analysis further in that context.

10. Emphasis in original; for some reason Street adds "to find" before "a baby"—this is not present in the original.

11. The story we have not discussed is a brief moral tale in which a young girl discovers the dangers of lying, a tale Street compares to Ruskin's "Sesame and Lilies": "Bram Stoker's succinct treatment of the propriety of a girl's learning and moral development . . . bear[s] a title similar to *Sesame and Lilies*, that longer work of Ruskin's. . . . The education and development of the female contains numerous pitfalls, it seems, the consequences of which appear more dire than for the male because of the frailties [*sic*] embraced by the former" (p. cvi).

## Chapter Four

1. In a fascinating study of the genre of *The Fantastic* (Cleveland: Press of Case Western Reserve University, 1973), Tsvetan Todorov divides into two major rubrics the themes of the genre: themes of the self and themes of the other. In the former, a "principle . . . of the fragility of the limit between matter and mind . . . engenders several fundamental themes," including "multiplication of the personality" (p. 120). However, in Stoker's work, the doubling typically is that of a character other than the subject; consequently, the second category Todorov defines includes those themes most relevant to Stoker's fiction for, as Todorov describes this rubric, it articulates a link between sexual desire and death, frequently manifested in themes of incest, necrophilia or vampirism.

2. First published in 1903; the text used here is the London, 1966 edition; hereafter cited in the text as *J.*

3. See E. A. Wallis Budge, *The Gods of the Egyptians, or Studies in Egyptian Mythology*, vol. 2 (New York: Dover, 1969). p. 299.

4. "Frère" being French for brother, the naming of the character here suggests both doubling (with Mr. Trelawny) and an association with Stoker's brother, Sir Wm. Thornley Stoker, the physician, whom Stoker consulted for the medical facts in his novels.

5. We recall the name "Daw" from "How 7 Went Mad" in *Under the Sunset.*

6. *The Jewel of Seven Stars* was published in an admittedly "abridged" version by Ann Reit (New York: Scholastic Book Services, 1972) which is also revised, in particular at the ending, which may reflect a dissatisfaction with the dénouement shared by this author as well. Reit chooses an uncharacteristic resolution for a Stoker novel, killing off all but Malcolm Ross.

More apposite here, readers familiar with H. Rider Haggard's *She* which first appeared in 1886 (and which C. G. Jung cites as an instance of the portrayal of the archetypal feminine) will detect not a few resemblances between Haggard's goddess Ayesha and Queen Tera. Ayesha, while remaining alive over the centuries, has also awaited her beloved who, in this case, appears in his double. She-who-must-be-obeyed also undergoes a dusty dissolution at the novel's resolution, and *The Jewel of Seven Stars* may be regarded as an inverted version of *She.*

7. Ludlam, p. 123.

8. The text used here is the London, 1966 edition; hereafter cited in the text as *L.*

9. Reminiscent of the bizarre fastidiousness and implicit prurience of *The Man*, Stoker details both a screen behind which Teuta changes to warm clothing and the sounds made by her wet cerements hitting the floor.

10. Freud speaks of rescue fantasies in several contexts: in his essay on "Creative Writers and Day-Dreaming" (1908) and in "A Special Type of Choice of Object Made by Men (Contributions to the Psychology of Love I)" (1910), volumes 9 and 11, respectively, of *The Standard Edition of the Complete Psychological Works of Sigmund Freud*, trans. James Strachey (London, 1962). The component of hostility in the fantasies is described more explicitly by Otto Rank

in *The Myth of the Birth of the Hero*, ed. Philip Freund (New York: Vintage Books, 1964), pp. 75ff. The psychoanalytic implications of the rescue fantasies depicted in Stoker's fiction will be explored more fully in the discussion of *Dracula* which follows.

11. The text used here is the London, 1966 edition; hereafter cited in the text as *W*.

*Chapter Five*

1. I am grateful to the director of the Rosenbach Library and Museum for permission to quote from these papers. In addition to the notes, the Rosenbach owns a presentation copy of *Dracula*, inscribed by Stoker "To the Right Honorable Lord Tennyson."

As a "List of Sources," Stoker noted the following: Sabine Baring-Gould, *Curious Myths of the Middle Ages* (London: Longmans, Green, 1901), *Germany Past and Present* (London: Kegan Paul, Trench, 1881), and *The Book of Were-Wolves* (London: Smith, Elder, 1865); Fletcher S. Bassett, *Legends and Superstitions of the Sea and of Sailors in All Lands at All Times* (Chicago: Belford, Clarke, 1885); Rushton M. Dorman, *The Origin of Primitive Superstitions* (Philadelphia: Lippicott, 1881); *John Jones, *The Natural and Supernatural*; W. Jones, *Credulities Past and Present* (London: Chatto & Windus, 1898) and *History and Mystery of Precious Stones* (London: R. Bentley & Son, 1880); *Rev. W. H. Jones, *Magyar Folk Tales*; Henry Charles Lea, *Superstition and Force* (Philadelphia: H. C. Lea, 1878); Sarah Lee, *Ancedotes of Habits and Instincts of Birds* (Philadelphia: Lindsay Blalmston, 1853). Frederick G. Lee, *The Other World* (London: H. S. King, 1875); *Maury (in French); Herbert Mayo, *Letters on the Truths Contained in Popular Superstition* (Frankfurt: J. D. Saverlander, 1849); *T. J. Pettigrew, *Superstitions Connected with History and Medicine*; *Reville. *History of the Devil*; *Sir T. Browner. *Necromancy—divination by the dead.*

The references with an asterisk are directly quoted from Stoker's notes. The others have been corrected to reflect available bibliographic information.

Stoker's notes also include a reference to "*Round about the Carpathians* by A. F. Crosse (Blackwoods 1878)"; notes on "robber steak," hayricks in trees, dangerous dogs in Hungary, the Czygany (Gypsies); a description of a *leitwagen*; a memo to himself that "horses are to be disturbed at approach of Count Dracula and smell blood!"; a reference to *"On the Track of the Crescent* by Major C. Johnson (Hurst and Blackett 1885)" from which Stoker noted details of women's clothing and a "Mamaliga" or pudding; and a reference to *"Transylvania* by Charles Couver (Longmans 1865)". Moreover, Stoker cites as a "Turkish proverb": "Water sleeps, and the Enemy is sleepless." Much of the above is familiar to the reader of *Dracula*. Finally, Stoker lists as a reference, and took extensive notes from, Mme. E. de Laszowska Gerard, "Transylvanian Superstitions," *XIX Century* 23 (July 1885): 130–50, an article which grew into the often cited *The Land Beyond the Forest*, author listed here as Emily Gerard.

2. The most extensive and scholarly discussions of Vlad the Impaler appear in two books by Radu Florescu and Raymond T. McNally, professors of history at Boston College: *In Search of Dracula* (New York, 1976) and *Dracula: A Biography of Vlad the Impaler, 1431–1476* (New York, 1973). Florescu and McNally identify the Impaler with Dracula, Vlad III. More exclusively concerned both with what he calls the "Dracula Myth"—that is, the way in which vampire legends and the stories of Vlad converge—and with identifying the "real" historical vampire (a Countess Elisabeth Báthory) (see note 69), Gabriel Ronay, in *The Truth about Dracula* (New York, 1979) says that "Philologists agreed at the Sixth Congress of Onomastic Sciences [at Munich, 1958] that Stoker's Dracula can be identified without a shadow of a doubt with Vlad V, called the Impaler, though it was his father, Vlad III, who was the first Wallachian ruler to be called 'Dracula'" (p. 58). However, according to Florescu and McNally, "Vlad V, or Vladut, spent all his early years at the monastery [at Snagov, where Dracula is reputedly interred] before becoming prince in 1530." His son, "yet another Vlad, known to history as Vlad VII, 'the Drowned,' . . . briefly ruled between 1530 and 1532. . . ." At least two Vlads apparently never ruled.

In a lengthy article entitled "The History of *Dracula:* The Theme of His Legend in the Western and Eastern Literatures of Europe" (*Comparative Literature Studies* 3 [1966]: 367–96), Grigor Nandris agrees with Ronay that the Vlad who was the Impaler was Vlad V. Nandris, however, acknowledges that another view exists. In any event, all agree on the deeds of Dracula, if not on which Vlad was the Impaler.

According to Florescu and McNally, "The dragon with wings biting its own tail was the insignia of Dracula's Order of the Dragon. The dragon has generally stood for 'things animal' and hence 'the adversary' par excellence. In Christian mythology the dragon is also specifically the evil symbol of Satan, which can also correspond with Dracula's evil image. In Romania the dragon is occasionally typified as a huge monster with two fantastic open jaws, one trailing the earth, the other high up, on the horizon, gulping everything in his way" (p. 176). If Stoker was aware of this iconography, he certainly would have found it appealing (recall, especially, the depictions of terrifying animals in "The Wondrous Child" from *Under the Sunset*).

3. Grigor Nandris, in the article cited above, argues persuasively that while most of the elements of the Dracula history and all of the vampire lore in *Dracula* actually exist, they have been considerably reworked by the novelist. Moreover, "the Dracula story did not penetrate into the Rumanian vampire tradition. It was Bram Stoker who transformed Dracula into a vampire" (p. 369). Nandris tells us, too, that one of the early incunabula on the historical Dracula had been owned by the British Museum—where, like Jonathan Harker, Stoker did his research—since 1846.

However, according to Florescu and McNally's discussion of Arminius Vambery, mentioned in *Dracula* as a source for Stoker,

Vambery himself was certainly familiar with Engel's *History of Moldavia and Wallachia*, in which there was a specific inclusion of the Dracula pamphlet in the National Museum in Budapest which portrayed Dracula as a berserker, a bloodthirsty monster. Vambery was not only familiar with the consistent image of Dracula as an arch villain and clever ruler in Hungarian folklore and history, but also knew that Hungarian vampire stories often associated the word "Dracul" with acts of vampirism. In fact, in 1886 the publication of an article identifying the word "Dracul" with vampire stories may have lent impetus to Vambery's influence on Stoker. (p. 151)

4. Florescu and McNally, p. 68.

5. Ibid., pp. 74–75.

6. Stoker indicates he is quoting from an "Account of the Principalities of Wallachia and Moldavia, etc. by Wm. Wilkinson, late counsul of Bukorest (Longmans 1820) Whitby Library 0.1097."

7. See Ronay's analysis, p. 48. Among the materials at the Rosenbach is a clipping of an article from the *New York World*, dated Sun-
day, 2 February 1896, headed "Vampires in New England—Dead
Bodies Dug Up and Their Hearts Burned to Prevent Disease." The
article discusses the discovery of vampire superstition in Rhode Island
as a result of which people who had died of consumption were dug up
so their hearts could be burned. The article also reports an epidemic
of vampires in Europe during the years 1727–35 (rather a late news
item), proposes an explanation in the possibility of live burial, and
concludes by explaining the latest scientific understanding of vampire
bats.

8. *A Biography of Vlad the Impaler*, p. 160.

9. Eino Railo, *The Haunted Castle* (London, 1927), pp. 200–201.

10. Ibid., pp. 197–98.

11. *Carmilla* (New York: Warner Books, 1974), pp. 25–26.

12. Ibid., p. 82.

13. See Mario Praz, *The Romantic Agony* (London: Oxford University Press, 1970), especially the chapter entitled "La Belle Dame
sans Merci."

14. The story is reprinted in *The Bram Stoker Bedside Companion:
10 Stories by the author of Dracula*, ed. Charles Osborne (New York,
1973), along with "The Invisible Giant" from *Under the Sunset* and
"The Gombeen Man," an excerpt from *The Snake's Pass*. The other
stories, some of them rather Poe-ish in their Gothicism, are well worth
reading.

15. Some of the notes are dated during 1895 and 1896 as well, so
Stoker seems to have worked for a full six years on *Dracula*, suggesting
that, rather than an anomalous achievement for him, *Dracula* indicates
his capabilities given the time and interest.

16. The edition used here, published by Rider & Co. in London, is
undated; it probably appeared shortly after Stoker's death.

17. *The Gothic Tradition in Fiction*, p. 22.

18. Ibid., pp. 4, 5.

19. This is certainly the argument of Thomas Ray Thornburg, "The
Quester and the Castle: The Gothic Novel as Myth, with Special Reference to Bram Stoker's *Dracula*" (Ph.D. diss., Ball State University,
1970; available through University Microfilms, Ann Arbor, Michigan).

20. Three articles in particular deal in fascinating ways with the
effect on the reader of the Gothic, especially the Gothic castle (pic-

tures of several Gothic cathedrals are among Stoker's papers at the Rosenbach): Claire Kahane, "Gothic Mirrors and Feminine Identity," *Centennial Review* 24, no. 1 (Winter 1980): 43–64; Norman N. Holland and Leona F. Sherman, "Gothic Possibilties," *New Literary History* 8, no. 2 (Winter 1977): 279–94; Philip P. Hallie, "Horror and the Paradox of Cruelty," *Monday Evening Papers*, no. 16 (Middletown, Conn., 1969). Hallie comments that "by heightening the strength of the strong one and by rendering the victim more passive, the castle helps generate and maintain the difference of power that helps make cruelty, like a spark of electricity, possible. The castle is the dynamo of cruelty" (p. 9).

21. In his essay on "The Uncanny" (in *The Complete Psychological Works of Sigmund Freud*, trans. James Strachey, vol. 17 [London, 1962], pp. 217–52), which is especially important for analyses of the Gothic, Freud argues that the sense of uncanniness is created by a nexus of themes, all of which are relevant to *Dracula*: for example, the perception of doubling, arousing "an uncanny feeling which, furthermore, recalls the sense of helplessness experienced in some dream states" (p. 237); our uncertainty about the firmness of the boundary between life and death; the widespread terror of being buried alive. Moreover, the uncanny is manifested in superstitions such as "the dread of the evil eye" (p. 240). There is, according to Freud, one essential condition for uncanniness: "An uncanny experience occurs either when infantile complexes which have been repressed are once more revived by some impression, or when primitive beliefs which have been surmounted seem once more to be confirmed" (p. 249). Thus, the uncanny arises from the return of the repressed, specifically and frequently, repressed infantile incestuous longings.

Moreover, as a noteworthy addendum here, Freud maintains that, "whenever a man dreams of a place or a country and says to himself, while he is still dreaming: 'this place is familiar to me, I've been here before', we may interpret this place as being his mother's genitals or her body" (p. 245). This analysis is explored with specific reference to the Gothic castle in Claire Kahane's article mentioned in note 20 and is one which complements our later discussion of the primary focus of *Dracula*.

22. Leonard Wolf, *The Annotated Dracula* (New York, 1975), p. 27. In MacAndrew's words, "the figure of the vampire is even farther from the human [than ghosts]. A grotesque that refuses to yield itself

to direct symbolic interpretation, it has a correspondingly greater suggestive power. A polymorphous, protean monster that drains the blood of the innocent, it is an embodiment of evil of special interest in Gothic fiction because of the decidedly sexual nature of its suggestiveness" (p. 166).

23. MacAndrew, p. 48.

24. For the most extensive study of this phenomenon, see Edward Said, *Orientalism* (New York: Pantheon Books, 1978). In an excitingly original article entitled "*Dracula*: The Gnostic Quest and Victorian Wasteland" (*English Literature in Translation* 20 [1977]: 13–26), Mark M. Hennelly, Jr. argues that the East/West opposition includes the opposition between two types of wasteland—"nocturnal-lunar Transylvania and diurnal-solar London"—each requiring the other for fertilization just as the "child-brain" of Dracula seeks the "man brains" of the hero, and indeed of Mina (p. 14); and that *Dracula* is an allegorical rendering of the oppositions between two types of wasteland and of the quest from each to the other.

25. MacAndrew, p. 165.

26. Ibid., p. 81.

27. An earlier version of the following analysis of *Dracula* appeared as "Suddenly Sexual Women in Bram Stoker's *Dracula*," *Literature and Psychology* 27, no. 3 (1972): 113–21.

28. Royce MacGillvray, "*Dracula*: Bram Stoker's Spoiled Masterpiece," *Queen's Quarterly* 79 (Winter 1972): 518.

29. See Norman N. Holland, *The Dynamics of Literary Response* (New York: Norton, 1975).

30. Maurice Richardson, "The Psychoanalysis of Ghost Stories," *Twentieth Century* 166 (December 1959): 427.

31. Richardson, p. 419, refers to Freud's observation that "morbid dread always signifies repressed sexual wishes."

32. C. F. Bentley, "The Monster in the Bedroom: Sexual Symbolism in Bram Stoker's *Dracula*," *Literature and Psychology* 22, no. 1 (1972): 29.

33. Joseph S. Bierman, "*Dracula*: Prolonged Childhood Illness and the Oral Triad," *American Imago* 29 (Summer 1972): 194.

34. Bentley, p. 28.

35. Richardson, p. 427.

36. MacGillvray, p. 522.

37. Richardson, p. 428. The Oedipal fantasy of the destruction of

the father is reinforced by a number of additional, and seemingly gratuitous, paternal deaths in the novel. See also MacGillvray, p. 523.

38. Richardson, p. 428. One cannot help but observe in the context that Bram's name was short for Abraham, the name of his father.

39. See, for instance, Richardson, p. 427. Wolf asks us to "note, too, that Lucy is getting the wish she made when she cried, 'Why can't they let a girl marry three men, or as many as want her, and save all this trouble?'" (p. 158).

40. Richard Wasson, "The Politics of *Dracula*," *English Literature in Translation* 9, no. 1 (1966): 24–27.

41. Ibid., p. 26.

42. Freud, *Totem and Taboo*, trans. James Strachey, in *The Standard Edition of the Complete Psychological Works of Sigmund Freud*, vol. 13 (1913–14) (London, 1962), pp. 37ff. For Freud's discussion of projection as a defense, see pp. 60–63.

43. Wolf, p. 267.

44. "Mina takes over and becomes everyone's bride, including, in time, Dracula's. What we have here is a matronly parallel to the scene in which Lucy receives three proposals, accepts one, and wishes she could accept all" (Wolf, p. 206).

45. Wolf, too, observes the change in Lucy's hair color and while he does not account for it, he does link her blondness to the mysterious face Jonathan sees: "This is a major mystery in the book. Whose face is it? There is the smallest hint that this blonde beauty may have something in common with Lucy . . . but see Chapter XVI . . . where Lucy is described as dark-haired" (p. 39).

46. See Carrol Fry, "Fictional Convention and Sex in *Dracula*," *Victorian Newsletter* 42 (Fall 1972). For further analysis of the prevalence of the Gothic light/dark heroines and their place and symbolic significance in the English literary tradition, see Elizabeth MacAndrew and Susan Gorsky, "Why Do They Faint and Die?—The Birth of the Delicate Heroine," *Journal of Popular Culture* 8 (Spring 1975): 735–45.

47. Stephanie Demetrakopoulos, "Feminism, Sex Role Exchanges, and Other Subliminal Fantasies in Bram Stoker's *Dracula*," *Frontiers* 2 (1977): 107. Demetrakopoulos also maintains that this "collective fantasy" of female sexual aggressiveness was expressive of Victorian ennui with conventional sex roles, an argument less convincing to us than that of the fear of the devouring mother. Judith Weissman

("Women and Vampires: *Dracula* as a Victorian Novel," *Midwest Quarterly* 18, 1977: 392–405), argues that "voraciously sexual women" existed in English literature long before Stoker but only with Stoker's vampires (and, as an exception to the generalization, *Jane Eyre*'s Bertha) are they clearly portrayed as terrifying. In contending that the primary threat of the novel is sexualized woman, Weissman observes that Dracula's threat is power, specifically the power to unleash female sexuality. In an article already cited, Mark Hennelly perceives Mina as the androgynous hero of the allegorical quest in *Dracula* who can give birth to a new king in whose blood hers mingles with that of both her husbands, Jonathan Harker and Dracula.

48. MacAndrew, pp. 167, 230.

49. One of the contexts in which Freud discusses the rescue motif in fantasy, a motif we have seen repeatedly in Stoker's fiction, is in his 1910 essay on "A Special Type of Choice of Object Made by Men" (which is usefully read with another essay also subtitled "Contributions to the Psychology of Love," this one entitled "On the Universal Tendency to Debasement in the Sphere of Love"). The situation Freud describes is one in which, as a consequence of an unresolved and unusually strong fixation on the mother, the male splits women into two opposite groups, mother and prostitute, the first of which engages his feelings of affection and respect, the second elicits his sensuality. In the second of the essays, Freud indicates that this splitting is a defense occasioned by the incest taboo which, internalized, causes the sensual feelings awakened by the mother to be repressed, or displaced. Repressed, too, is the awareness the little boy has gained of his mother's sexual experiences. Around the same time, according to Freud, that is, prior to puberty, the boy becomes aware that certain women receive money for these sexual favors.

In the first of the two essays referred to, Freud describes one manifestation of this situation: in this case, the boy makes the connection between mother's activities with father and those of the prostitute. His response may then be the desire to "rescue" the mother from what is perceived as her tendency to "fall" into "sin." For Freud, however, this explanation is in fact a rationalization, screening the actual and unconscious motive of the rescue fantasy which has to do with the boy's desire to reciprocate the mother's life-giving relation to him. "The son shows his gratitude by wishing to have by his mother a son who is like himself: in other words, in the rescue-phantasy he is completely identifying himself with his father" (*Standard Edition*, 11: 173). (The hostile component of the rescue fantasy, as we have indicated elsewhere, is more extensively described in Otto Rank's essay on "The Myth of the Birth of the Hero," a fuller discussion of the "neurotic family romance" Freud mentions in the essay under discussion here.) All of these elements appear in *Dracula*, as well as in the early story from *Under the Sunset*, "The Wondrous Child."

An additional manifestation of the incestuous fixation on the mother, described by Freud in the second essay, develops as a marked and sustained split between the mother and the prostitute images, as a consequence of which the male "overvalues" the woman whom he sees to resemble the mother, but is impotent with her. In this situation, the male can only enjoy his sensuality with a woman whom he perceives as debased; indeed, only she is perceived as a sexualized woman. It is possible, though not ascertainable, that this dilemma describes Stoker's sex life; certainly it would explain the events leading to Stoker's degenerative illness and death as described by Daniel Farson.

What Freud describes in these essays characterizes a typical manifestation of the sexual lives of the Victorians (see also Stephen Marcus, *The Other Victorians: A Study of Sexuality and Pornography in Mid-Nineteenth-Century England* (New York, 1974).

50. In a beautifully written piece entitled "Night Thoughts on the Gothic Novel" (*Yale Review* 52 [1963]: 236–57), Lowry Nelson, Jr., similarly claims: "By its insistence on singularity and exotic setting, the gothic novel seems to have freed the minds of readers from direct involvement of their superegos and allowed them to pursue day dreams and wish fulfillment in regions where inhibition and guilt could be suspended" (p. 238).

51. Wolf observes that "Mina" is almost "anima," or soul (p. 264).

52. Wolf, who also marvels at this cruelty (p. 276), claims that "Mina echoes the Victorian (and not yet wholly altered) masculine view that the rape victim was morally stained by the violent embrace she endured. Though Jonathan Harker rejects the notion, the rest of the action of the book is predicated on its force. Mina has been stained, spotted" (p. 252).

53. "One could argue that, beginning with Professor Van Helsing's secrecy, all the catastrophes of the book . . . have come about because of unshared confidence" (Wolf, p. 258).

54. Bentley, pp. 29–30; MacGillvray, p. 522.

55. Bentley, p. 30.

56. Bierman, p. 194. Bierman's analysis, as we have seen earlier, is concerned to demonstrate that "*Dracula* mirrors Stoker's early childhood . . ." and is a highly speculative but fascinating study. The emphasis is on Stoker's rivalry with his brothers but it provides, albeit indirectly, further evidence of hostility toward the rejecting mother.

57. Ludlam cites one of the actors in the Hamilton Deane stage production of *Dracula* as indicating that the adaptation was so successful that " 'Disturbances in the circle or stalls as people felt faint and had to be taken out were not uncommon—and they were perfectly genuine, not a publicity stunt. Strangely enough, they were generally men' " (p. 165).

58. "Sharp-pointed instruments seem to be sexually totemic for the men in this book. The weapons, in order of increasing size, are as follows: Seward carries a lancet; Quincy Morris will be armed with a bowie knife; Jonathan Harker with a kukri knife; and Dr. Van Helsing, their teacher, produces, when the time comes, the most formidable weapon of all—the stake" (Wolf, p. 60).

59. In the terms of Philip Hallie's argument, "the curious fact remains that these Romantic-sensationalistic novels glorify the power of the victim, and glorify especially her power to victimize her victimizer. Here . . . , the moral and the esthetic come together (in a successful Gothic tale) to produce an esthetic *cum* moral consummation" (p. 26). In the terms of the present analysis, the fact is not at all curious. Moreover, devotees of the horror tale will recall both the ending of the original *Nosferatu*, in which the heroine destroys the villain and the original film of *King Kong* which ends with the line, " 'Twas beauty killed the beast."

Gabriel Ronay's analysis of vampirism is tied up with this peculiar though not unique conception of female sexuality, one he sees manifest in the very earliest of vampire tales: "A type of female vampire that used the pleasures of lovemaking to ensnare handsome youths and drain them of blood and devour them, was greatly feared in ancient Greece. Philostratus in his *Life of Apollonius* describes a classic case of erotic vampirism, revealing the sources of the belief in this particular species of the *genus vampiricus*: man's primordial sexual fear of the woman who initiates and then devours (castrates) the male as she received him" (p. 5). Indeed, Ronay expends considerable effort to straighten out the history of Vlad the Impaler who, while noteworthy for his sexually tinged atrocities against enemies and compatriots alike, in his lifetime impaling thousands of victims in all manner of hideous postures, was not a vampire according to Ronay. Rather the true vampire was one Countess Elisabeth Báthory, a "famous society beauty and offspring of one of the ancient European aristocratic families" (p. 94) living in the Carpathians in the early seventeenth century. According to the trial transcripts and depositions Ronay cites, Elisabeth Báthory was responsible for the brutal murders of six hundred and fifty girls whose blood she required for purportedly rejuvenating bloodbaths. Though Ronay acknowledges that Elisabeth Báthory was heterosexual, he accounts in part for her sadism by reference to an initiation she received while visiting "her aunt, the Countess Klara Báthory, a well-known lesbian" (p. 102). Thus, Ronay concludes, Elisabeth received support in acting out "her sadistic lesbian fantasies" (p. 96). Indeed, for him, there is a sort of equation between lesbianism and vampirism, an identification shared both by Sheridan Le Fanu in *Carmilla* and by the makers of many contemporary pornographic vampire films. Ronay claims of *Carmilla* that "Le Fanu sketched in convincing detail the lesbian root of real life vampirism" (p. 126).

60. See, for instance, Wolfgang Lederer, M.D., *The Fear of Women* (New York: Harcourt Brace Jovanovich, 1968), especially the chapter entitled, "A Snapping of Teeth."

61. Otto Rank, *The Trauma of Birth* (New York: Harper & Row, 1973), p. 73.

62. When discussing the present analysis with a class, two of my students argued that Dracula is not, in fact, destroyed at the novel's conclusion. They maintained that his last look is one of triumph and that his heart is not staked but pierced by a mere bowie knife. Their suggestion that, at least, the men do not follow the elaborate procedures to insure the destruction of Dracula that they religiously observe with regard to that of the women, is certainly of value here, whether one agrees that Dracula still stalks the land. My thanks to Lucinda Donnelly and Barbara Kotacka for these observations.

63. Wolf, p. 255, xviii.

64. Hallie, p. 15.

65. To explore further the Gothic impulse among the Romantics, see *The Gothic Imagination: Essays in Dark Romanticism,* ed. G. R. Thompson (Pullman, Washington: Washington State University

Press, 1974). For an exploration of the vampire in Romanticism, see James B. Twitchell, *The Living Dead: A Study of the Vampire in Romantic Literature* (Durham, N.C., 1981).

66. Wolf, p. xv.

*Chapter Six*

1. For the full development of this analysis see Charles S. Blinderman, "Vampurella: Darwin and Count Dracula," *Massachusetts Review*, Summer 1980, pp. 411–28.

2. *Famous Imposters* (New York, 1910), p. v; hereafter cited in the text as *F*.

3. Quoted in Laurence Irving, *Henry Irving: The Actor and His World* (New York: Macmillan, 1952), p. 452.

4. Ibid., p. 480.

# Selected Bibliography

PRIMARY SOURCES

1. Novels

*Dracula*. Westminster: A. Constable, 1897. Currently available in both
Dell and Signet paperbacks and in *The Annotated Dracula*, with
introduction, notes, and bibliography by Leonard Wolf, art by
Sätty (New York: Ballantine, 1976).
*The Jewel of Seven Stars*. 1903. Reprint. London: Jarrolds, 1966.
*Lady Athlyne*. New York: Paul R. Reynolds, 1908.
*The Lady of the Shroud*. 1909. Reprint. London: Jarrolds, 1966.
*The Lair of the White Worm*. 1911. Reprint. London: Jarrolds, 1966.
*The Man*. London: Heinemann, 1905.
*Miss Betty*. 1898. Reprint. London: New English Library, 1974.
*The Mystery of The Sea*. 1902. Reprint. London: Rider, n.d.
*The Snake's Pass*. 1890. Reprint. London: Collier, 1909.

2. Collected Stories

*The Bram Stoker Bedside Companion: Ten Stories by the Author of
Dracula*. Edited by Charles Osborne. New York: Taplinger, 1973.
Includes: "The Secret of Growing Gold," "Dracula's Guest,"
"The Invisible Giant," "The Judge's House," "The Burial of
the Rats," "A Star Trap," "The Squaw," "Crooken Sands," "The
Gombeen Man," "The Watter's Mou'."
*Under the Sunset*. London: Sampson, Low, Marston, Searle, and Riv-
ington, 1882. Available also in Douglas Oliver Street, *Bram
Stoker's "Under the Sunset": An Edition with Introductory Bio-
graphical and Critical Material* (Ph.D. dissertation, University of
Nebraska 1977). Paperback issued by Newcastle Publishers,
1978.

## 3. Nonfiction

*Famous Imposters.* New York: Sturgis & Walton, 1910.
*Personal Reminiscences of Henry Irving.* 2 vols. London: Macmillan, 1906.

## 4. Manuscripts

Philadelphia. Rosenbach Museum and Library. Seventy-eight pages of notes, outlines, and diagrams for *Dracula.*

## SECONDARY SOURCES

### 1. Biographies

FARSON, DANIEL. *The Man Who Wrote Dracula: A Biography of Bram Stoker.* New York: St. Martin's Press, 1976. A work primarily distinguished from Ludlam's biography, on which it relies heavily, by access to family materials which Farson, as Stoker's grandnephew, received from Noel Stoker. Otherwise undistinguished.

LUDLAM, HARRY. *A Biography of Dracula: The Life Story of Bram Stoker.* London: Foulsham, 1962. Despite the alluring title, a rather plodding, albeit useful, recounting of the events of Stoker's life with some plot summaries and criticism in passing.

### 2. Critical Studies

#### a. Books

FLORESCU, RADU, and McNALLY, RAYMOND T. *Dracula: A Biography of Vlad the Impaler, 1431–1476.* New York: Hawthorn Books, 1973. The most complete, thoroughly researched, and detailed account of the life of Count Dracula's prototype. Includes full listing of sources, both published and in manuscript, and a chapter on Vlad's literary descendants.
————. *In Search of Dracula.* New York: Warner Books, 1976. Originally published before the more scholarly history, this is a more popular analysis of both Vlad's and Stoker's stories. Included are translations of fifteenth-century stories about the

Impaler, a filmography of vampire films, and an annotated bibliography.

MACANDREW, ELIZABETH. *The Gothic Tradition in Fiction.* New York: Columbia University Press, 1979. Excellent study of the Gothic as genre, its tradition, its development, its outstanding characteristics, unified by the thesis that the Gothic is a "symbolic construct" enabling its practitioners to explore and make manifest psychic conflict.

MARCUS, STEPHEN. *The Other Victorians: A Study of Sexuality and Pornography in Mid-Nineteenth Century England.* New York: Basic Books, 1974. Fine exploration of striking duplicities, dichotomies, and ambivalences regarding sexuality, especially female, in Victorian England.

PATTISON, BARRIE. *The Seal of Dracula.* New York: Bounty Books, 1975. Essentially an annotated list and summary of the history of vampire films from the silent pictures through contemporary pornography.

RAILO, EINO. *The Haunted Castle: A Study of the Elements of English Romanticism.* London: George Routledge, 1927. An older and primarily thematic study of Gothic components, especially useful for the connections it draws between romantic poets and Gothic novelists.

RONAY, GABRIEL. *The Truth About Dracula.* New York: Day, 1979. A less than scholarly discussion of Vlad the Impaler. Ronay is more concerned to argue that the "real" vampire was a woman, Countess Elisabeth Báthory. Useful discussion of the prevalence and spread of vampire scares. No bibliography.

TWITCHELL, JAMES B. *The Living Dead: A Study of the Vampire in Romantic Literature.* Durham, N.C.: Duke University Press, 1981. A thoughtful and witty exploration of the prevalence and meanings of the vampire in the work of the major Romantic poets, in nineteenth century prose, and in James and Lawrence. Includes an overview of vampire legends and a brief history of Vlad the Impaler (though ignoring certain historical confusions), as well as a plot summary of *Varney, the Vampire.*

WOLF, LEONARD. *The Annotated Dracula* by Bram Stoker. Introduction, notes, and bibliography by Leonard Wolf. New York: Ballantine Books, 1975. This book is for the *Dracula* fan. Wolf painstakingly notes much of interest from recipes for chicken paprika

and uses for garlic to Shakespearean allusions in *Dracula*. Biographically oriented introduction is cursory, but the book includes
maps of central locations in *Dracula*, the calendar of the novel's
events, and a bibliography.

————. *A Dream of Dracula*. New York: Popular Library, 1972.
An extended meditation on the prevalence of the archetypal
imagery of nightmare, focusing in particular on blood lust and
rites and on the terror of death. Wolf sets *Dracula* in a large
context, and glides smoothly from the biblical stories of Lilith,
Abraham and Isaac, and Cain, to Hell's Angels initiation rituals
and to the Gothic tradition, helpfully clarifying the distinctive-
ness of Stoker's work. Apparently motivated by a midlife crisis in
coming to terms with mortality, the book is somewhat marred
by a maudlin and narcissistic fascination with the author's own
blood.

## b. Articles

BENTLEY, C. F. "The Monster in the Bedroom: Sexual Symbolism in
Bram Stoker's *Dracula*." *Literature and Psychology* 22, no. 1
1972): 27–33. An early and important essay demonstrating that
the vampirism in *Dracula* is transformed sexuality.

BIERMAN, JOSEPH S. "Dracula: Prolonged Childhood Illness and the
Oral Triad." *American Imago* 29 (1972): 186–98. Correlation
of two early Stoker stories from *Under the Sunset* with *Dracula*,
with Stoker's childhood, and with Bertram Lewin's "Oral Triad":
the wish to eat, be eaten and sleep."

————. "The Genesis and Dating of *Dracula* from Bram Stoker's
Working Notes." *Notes and Queries*, n.s. 24, no. 1 (1977):
39–41: Asserting the inadequacy of previous accounts (by Ludlam and Florescu and McNally) of the genesis of *Dracula*, Bierman employs Stoker's notes at the Rosenbach to date the novel's
inception as early as 1890 and indicates that Stoker's research at
Whitby introduced him to the historical Dracula as early as that
year.

BLINDERMAN, CHARLES S., "Vampurella: Darwin and Count Dracula." *Massachusetts Review*, Summer 1980, pp. 411–28. A new
approach to *Dracula* which argues persuasively that Stoker's
novel reflects the Victorian conflict between philosophical and

religious dualism on the one hand, and a reductionist materialism based on T. H. Huxley's extensions of Darwinism on the other.

CARLSON, M. M. "What Stoker Saw: An Introduction to the History of the Literary Vampire." *Folklore Forum* 10, no. 2 (1977): 26–32. Argues for the primacy of literary prototypes (rather than historical or folkloric), especially Polidori's *The Vampire, a Tale* and LeFanu's *Carmilla*. Also provides good summary of ninetenth-century European and English vampire tales.

DEMETRAKOPOULOS, STEPHANIE. "Feminism, Sex Role Exchanges, and Other Subliminal Fantasies in Bram Stoker's *Dracula*." *Frontiers* 111 (1977): 104–13. Adds a new dimension to the conventional readings of fair/dark heroines, arguing that in *Dracula* the vampire women are examples of sex role reversal.

FREUD, SIGMUND. "A Special Type of Choice of Object Made by Men" and "On the Universal Tendency to Debasement in the Sphere of Love." In *The Standard Edition of the Complete Edition of the Psychological Works of Sigmund Freud*, vol. 11. Translated by James Strachey. London: Hogarth Press, 1962. Both essays are invaluable for understanding the splitting of the female imago into two opposite types. The first essay discusses fantasies of rescue.

FRY, CARROL L. "Fictional Conventions and Sexuality in *Dracula*." *Victorian Newsletter* 42 (Fall 1972): 20–22. Discusses vampirism and sexuality as well as Dracula as both rake and Gothic villain in conventional pursuit of the pure woman of melodrama. Once caught, the pure woman becomes the fallen women.

HALLIE, PHILIP, P. "Horror and The Paradox of Cruelty." *Monday Evening Papers* no. 16. Middletown, Conn.: Wesleyan University, Center for Advanced Studies, 1969. Interesting essay on cruelty( part of a longer and more philosophically oriented work) which focuses on the reader's ambivalence toward victim and villain in horror tales.

HENNELLY, MARK M., JR. "*Dracula*: The Gnostic Quest and Victorian Wasteland." *English Literature in Transition* 20 (1977): 13–26. A superb allegorical reading of *Dracula* as a double quest myth in which the Van Helsing forces and Dracula each seek transfusions from the other in order to escape the barrenness of their respective wastelands.

MACANDREW, ELIZABETH, and GORSKY, SUSAN. "Why Do They

Faint and Die?—The Birth of the Delicate Heroine." *Journal of Popular Culture* 8 (Spring 1975): 735–45. Good analysis of light and dark heroines in the Gothic tradition, their roles and symbolic significance.

MACGILLVRAY, ROYCE. "*Dracula*: Bram Stoker's Spoiled Masterpiece." *Queen's Quarterly* 79 (1972): 518–27. Wishing to include *Dracula* in the canon of works for scholarly consideration, MacGillvray argues that it is a novel of alienation, of parricide, and of the murder of children by their parents, as well as a masterpiece spoiled by weak characterization and sentimentality.

NANDRIS, GRIGOR. "The History of Dracula: The Theme of His Legend in the Western and Eastern Literatures of Europe." *Comparative Literature Studies* 3 (1966): 367–96. Perhaps the most complete catalog and analysis of Dracula stories (written in several languages), this lengthy article more or less systematically describes the history of Vlad the Impaler and of folkloric traditions relevant to *Dracula*. Nandris has as his express purpose a presentation of the "interplay of literary history, literary criticism and of history itself."

NELSON, LOWRY, JR. "Night Thoughts on The Gothic Novel." *Yale Review* 52 (1963): 236–57. Like MacAndrew's, Nelson's analysis demonstrates the strength and uniqueness of the Gothic in symbolizing the mind at work and in conflict. The article is beautifully written.

RICHARDSON, MAURICE. "The Psychoanalysis of Ghost Stories." *Twentieth Century* 166 (December 1959): 419–31. An early and useful attempt to demonstrate the explanatory force of psychoanalytic theory in relation to the dread and fascination of the nightmarish tale. Discusses *Dracula* and others.

WASSON, RICHARD. "The Politics of *Dracula*." *English Literature in Transition* 9 (1966): 24–27. Argues that *Dracula* is, albeit covertly, a political novel in which Stoker depicts a battle between the older, intuitive, irrational forces of the East against the rational, technological forces of the West, dramatizing the threat to modern man of failing to acknowledge his own repressed irrationality.

WEISSMAN, JUDITH. "Women and Vampires: *Dracula* as a Victorian Novel." *Midwest Quarterly* 18 (1977): 392–405. Traces "voraciously sexual women" through English literature and argues that only in *Dracula* and in one or two other isolated cases are these characters and their sexuality portrayed as truly terrifying, an interesting though not particularly accurate assessment.

# Index

**DATE DUE**

| AP 26 '85 | MAY 10 '85 | | |
|---|---|---|---|
| | | | |
| | | | |
| | | | |
| | | | |
| | | | |
| | | | |
| | | | |
| | | | |
| | | | |
| | | | |
| | | | |
| | | | |
| | | | |
| | | | |

DEMCO 38-297